LOVE THAT REJOICES
in the **TRUTH**

LOVE THAT REJOICES
in the **TRUTH**

THEOLOGICAL EXPLORATIONS

Charles M. Wood

CASCADE *Books* · Eugene, Oregon

LOVE THAT REJOICES IN THE TRUTH
Theological Explorations

Copyright © 2009 Charles M. Wood. All rights reserved. Except for brief quotations in critical publications or reviews, no part of this book may be reproduced in any manner without prior written permission from the publisher. Write: Permissions, Wipf and Stock Publishers, 199 W. 8th Ave., Suite 3, Eugene, OR 97401.

Cascade Books
A Division of Wipf and Stock Publishers
199 W. 8th Ave., Suite 3
Eugene, OR 97401

www.wipfandstock.com

ISBN 13: 978-1-55635-953-8

Cataloging-in-Publication data:

Wood, Charles Monroe.

    Love that rejoices in the truth : theological explorations / Charles M. Wood.

    x + 156 p. ; 20 cm. — Includes bibliographical references.

    ISBN 13: 978-1-55635-953-8

    1. Theology—Study and teaching. 2. United Methodist Church (U.S.)—Doctrines. 3. Bible Criticism, interpretation, etc. I. Title

BT28 .W66 2009

Manufactured in the U.S.A.

CONTENTS

Preface • vii

Acknowledgments • ix

1 Methodist Doctrine: An Understanding • 1

2 Wesleyan Constructive Theology • 23

3 The Primacy of Scripture • 35

4 Word of God and Truth • 43

5 Scripture, Authenticity, and Truth • 57

6 Theological Education: Confessional and Public • 83

7 Not Every School • 113

8 Paying Attention • 127

9 Rejoicing in the Truth • 135

Bibliography • 151

PREFACE

LOVE, SAYS THE apostle Paul, "does not rejoice over injustice, but rejoices in the truth" (1 Cor 13:6; my translation). Regrettably, rejoicing in the truth does not seem to come naturally to human beings in our present state. It might come naturally, were we not so thoroughly entangled in deceit and self-deception as to have become enemies of the truth rather than its friends. For us to become capable of welcoming truth, actively seeking it and rejoicing in it, requires a deep change. To undergo that change is to receive a life-transforming gift.

Like Paul and his contemporaries, generations of Christians have understood a new capacity for and disposition toward truth as something that belongs to the renewed human identity that is fashioned when "God's love has been poured into our hearts though the Holy Spirit that has been given to us" (Rom 5:5 NRSV). Of course, those same generations of Christians, up to and including our own, have given ample evidence that this renewal is at best fitful and incomplete, and that, generally speaking, the perfect love that casts out fear (1 John 4:18) does not yet govern our individual or corporate lives. Consequently, we remain conflicted about the truth; we have issues with it.

The theological explorations undertaken here all deal in one way or another with the liberating promise and the perplexing problem of truth in Christian life and witness, and with the ways that Christian theology and theological education in their various modes struggle both to seek the truth and to foster the aptitude to honor it. Several of these chapters were composed for specific occasions. Some are concerned to explicate insights and resources from the Wesleyan heritage or to address matters that have arisen more immediately in the United Methodist version of that tradition. Others have broader contexts and issues in view. My hope is that all of them might be of use to readers from a variety of Christian traditions and theological standpoints. Some of the chapters have been slightly revised for this collection, mainly in the interest of consistency in style.

CHARLES M. WOOD

ACKNOWLEDGMENTS

"Methodist Doctrine: An Understanding" was presented to the Systematic Theology Working Group at the Tenth Oxford Institute of Methodist Theological Studies in 1997, and was subsequently published in *Quarterly Review* 18:2 (Summer 1998) 167–82. Used with permission.

"Wesleyan Constructive Theology" was presented to a workgroup on Wesleyan Constructive Theology at the bicentennial theological consultation, "Wesleyan Theology in the Next Century," at Emory University in Atlanta in 1983. It was first published in the *Perkins Journal* 37 (Spring 1984) 12–17, and reprinted in the proceedings of the consultation, *Wesleyan Theology Today: A Bicentennial Theological Consultation*, edited by Theodore Runyon (Nashville: Kingswood Books, 1985).

"The Primacy of Scripture" was delivered at a gathering of ministers of the North Texas Annual Conference of the United Methodist Church in 2000 to consider that theme, and was first published in the *Perkins School of Theology Perspective* (Spring 2006) 16–17.

"Word of God and Truth" first appeared in *Encounter* 41 (1980) 219–27. Reprinted here, with slight revisions, with permission.

"Scripture, Authenticity, and Truth" was presented at a conference on the Bible and Theology at the Divinity School of the

University of Chicago in May 1995, and was first published in the *Journal of Religion* 76 (1996) 189–205.

"Theological Education: Confessional and Public" originated as two lectures for a consultation of the Associação de Seminários Teológicos Evangélicos in Brazil in December 1999. A Portuguese translation was published in the ASTE journal, *Simpósio* (São Paulo) 9:42 (2000) 5–22. The present English version was published online at Resources for American Christianity (http://www.resourcingchristianity.org) in 2001. Used here with permission.

"Not Every School" was delivered as the Colwell-Cranston Lecture at the Fall opening convocation of the School of Theology at Claremont in September 1994, and was subsequently published as the *School of Theology at Claremont Occasional Paper* 18 (September 1995).

"Paying Attention" was prepared in 1993 as a brief report on a consultation of church leaders on theological education funded by Lilly Endowment, Inc., and held under the auspices of the Center for the Study of Theological Education at Auburn Theological Seminary. It was published in *Quarterly Review* 13:3 (Fall 1993): 39–44. Used with permission.

"Rejoicing in the Truth" was published in *Quarterly Review* 24:2 (Summer 2004) 131–41. Used with permission.

1

METHODIST DOCTRINE: An Understanding

SOME TIME AGO, a theological colleague who is not a Methodist asked me what courses I was then teaching. When I told him I was teaching United Methodist Doctrine, his quiet response was, "That must be a short course." Methodists have a reputation among some other Christians for being short on doctrine, or doctrinally thin. It is widely believed that a walk through the Methodist doctrinal pond would hardly get one's feet wet. It is not only other Christians who have this impression of us, of course; many Methodists share it, and take it either as a point of pride (the dominant view, so far as I can see) or as a reason for self-reproach (a minority view, whose influence waxes and wanes periodically).

H. Richard Niebuhr once observed that debates about the authority of the Bible are unproductive when it is assumed that the question is a quantitative one ("How much authority does the Bible have?") rather than a qualitative one ("What kind of authority does it have?").[1] I believe that estimates of

1. See the introduction by James M. Gustafson in Niebuhr's *The Responsible Self*, 19–25.

Methodist doctrine often go astray for much the same reason. We readily fall into the quantitative way of thinking, and have earnest discussions about how much doctrine Methodists have, or should have. We would be helped by a clearer apprehension of what kind of doctrine Methodist doctrine is. My aim here is to work toward this clearer apprehension.

I believe that the standards of Methodist witness and practice, and particularly John Wesley's doctrinal sermons, convey an important insight into the character of Christian doctrine. By this, I do not mean to call attention to purportedly distinctive Methodist doctrines; on the whole, when it comes to the content of what Methodists believe and teach (or should believe and teach), I agree with those who find it more accurate to speak of distinctive Methodist doctrinal emphases, rather than distinctive doctrines.[2] But in any case, my main concern here is not with any distinctive content. Instead, I want to pursue a Wesleyan or Methodist understanding of the fundamental character of Christian doctrine as such, and a way of holding and deploying doctrine—you might say, a characteristic way of being doctrinal—that follows from that understanding. I believe that those of us who find ourselves within this particular stream of Christian tradition should explicate this insight and become more deliberate in our appropriation and representation of it, both for the sake of clarity as to what we are about doctrinally as Methodists and for the sake of the contribution this might make to the wider Christian community.

In his classic *The Meaning of Revelation*, written nearly sixty years ago, H. Richard Niebuhr writes:

2. See "Doctrinal Standards and Our Theological Task," in United Methodist Church, *Book of Discipline* (1996), 43.

A critical historical theology cannot, to be sure, prescribe what form religious life must take in all places and all times beyond the limits of its own historical system. But it can seek within the history of which it is a part for an intelligible pattern; it can undertake to analyze the reason which is in that history and to assist those who participate in this historical life to disregard in their thinking and practice all that is secondary and not in conformity with the central ideas and patterns of the historical movement. Such theology can attempt to state the grammar, not of a universal religious language, but of a particular language, in order that those who use it may be kept in true communication with each other and with the realities to which the language refers. It may try to develop a method applicable not to all religions but to the particular faith to which its historical point of view is relevant. Such theology in the Christian church cannot, it is evident, be an offensive or defensive enterprise which undertakes to prove the superiority of Christian faith to all other faiths; but it can be a confessional theology which carries on the work of self-criticism and self-knowledge of the church.[3]

What Niebuhr was advocating here, under the alternate names of a critical historical theology and a confessional theology, was an approach to theological work that took very seriously the "local knowledge" of a particular religious tradition and community, its own ways of knowing what it knows, its own access to reality, the "reason" informing its own life. Theology appropriately begins, not with an arrogant effort to

3. Niebuhr, *The Meaning of Revelation*, 13.

"make sense" of a religious tradition by subjecting it to supposedly universal standards of intelligibility, but rather with a patient attempt to learn and explicate the sense already present in it. That may not be all that theology has to do, but it is an indispensable beginning.

The notion that a religious tradition has something like a grammar has been around for quite some time. It was a familiar metaphor in medieval theology. Martin Luther is said (by J. A. Bengel and, following him, John Wesley) to have remarked that "divinity is nothing but a grammar of the language of the Holy Ghost."[4] The metaphor was given new life in certain strands of twentieth-century Anglo-American theology and philosophy of religion under the influence of Ludwig Wittgenstein's comparison of philosophical analysis to grammatical investigation,[5] and it gained wider currency with the publication of and reception of George Lindbeck's *The Nature of Doctrine*. It is now fairly common to hear doctrinal formulations compared to grammatical principles, catechesis compared to grammatical instruction, and theology described as an investigation of the grammar of the language and life of a religious community.

Some of the values of the metaphor are readily apparent. Just as "doctrine" can refer either to the technical principles formally stated in doctrinal pronouncements and handbooks, or to the embodiment of those principles in the teaching ac-

---

4. Wesley, *Explanatory Notes upon the New Testament*, 9.

5. A parenthetical remark in the midst of Wittgenstein's main discussion of his sense of "grammar" in the *Philosophical Investigations* is reminiscent of the statement Bengel attributed to Luther. "Grammar tells what kind of object anything is. (Theology as grammar.)" Wittgenstein, *Philosophical Investigations*, sec. 373.

tivity of the church and in the lives of its members, so "grammar" can designate either the formulated conventions of linguistic use, or the features of the language and of linguistic ability that those formulations codify. Grammatical formulations both describe and, in some circumstances, regulate the use of the language, but a competent speaker need not be able to formulate correctly the conventions he or she observes in exercising that competence. Conversely, a knowledge of the grammatical formulations does not insure competence in the language. Mastery of the language and conscious knowledge of the "rules" describing such mastery are two different things, and they do not always coincide. (Similarly, understanding Christian doctrinal formulations and understanding things Christianly are two different things.)

"Learning grammar" can mean either learning the grammatical formulations or acquiring competence in the language. If the aim is the latter, the former may have a quite limited role to play. Traditional approaches to second-language teaching overestimated their importance, emphasizing a mastery of the formulations and giving little attention to practice in listening and speaking the language itself. They appear to have been less effective in fostering actual linguistic ability than more recent approaches stressing exposure to the living language—hearing and imitating competent speakers, and having one's mistakes corrected, with only an occasional explicit invocation of grammatical principles.[6] (Similarly, teaching someone doctrinal formulations and teaching someone to understand things Christianly are two different things, and the role of the first in the second needs some careful pedagogical attention.)

6. Edwards, *Multilingualism*, 63–64.

Several contemporary theologians, utilizing this grammatical metaphor, have made a strong claim concerning the unique role of the doctrine of the Trinity in the language and life of the Christian community: namely, that it is the key element in Christian grammar, or (as one of them, Walter Kasper, puts it) "the doctrine of the Trinity is the grammar and summation of the entire Christian mystery of salvation."[7] According to these theologians, if we are to seek what Niebuhr calls "an intelligible pattern" in Christian faith and practice, it is to (or with the help of) the doctrine of the Trinity that we should look.

As an exploratory exercise, I want to pursue this suggestion with regard to one theme in the thought of John Wesley. I will call this theme Wesley's doctrine of the human vocation. (I am not aware of his ever having used that term, but it is useful in bringing out some connections.) But before turning to that theme, I need to say something about Wesley's approach to doctrine in general, and to the doctrine of the Trinity in particular.

Wesley's own attitude toward doctrine has long been a matter of contention, partly because of the varied character of his own pronouncements on the subject and partly because of the varied interests and commitments of his interpreters.[8] My

---

7. Kasper, *The God of Jesus Christ*, 311. Nicholas Lash, drawing on Kasper's work, has pursued this claim in some promising directions. See, for example, his *Believing Three Ways in One God: A Reading of the Apostles' Creed* and *The Beginning and the End of "Religion."* Thomas F. Torrance develops the point independently in *The Ground and Grammar of Theology*, esp. 154–57.

8. Randy Maddox has given us a very thorough, balanced, and illuminating treatment of Wesley's utterances on the subject, and of how they might be brought into a reasonably coherent relationship. Maddox, "Opinion, Religion, and 'Catholic Spirit,'" 63–87.

object here is not to go into this issue in any depth, but only to set out what I take to be Wesley's principal commitments. At a number of places in his writings, he made clear his conviction that religion (or "true religion") is not to be identified with doctrine or "opinion." (Though he occasionally distinguished between "doctrine" and "opinion," he often used these two terms as synonyms.) The point is made forcefully in his sermon on "The Way to the Kingdom": Having said that religion does not consist in "outward action," he continues:

> . . . neither does religion consist in *orthodoxy* or *right opinions*; which, although they are not properly outward things, are not in the heart, but the understanding. A man may be orthodox at every point; he may not only espouse right opinions, but zealously defend them against all opposers; he may think justly concerning the incarnation of our Lord, concerning the ever blessed Trinity, and every other doctrine contained in the oracles of God. He may assent to all the three Creeds . . . . He may be almost as orthodox as the devil . . . and may all the while be as great a stranger as he to the religion of the heart.[9]

The point is echoed and then supplemented in an important direction in the sermon "On the Trinity": "Persons may be quite right in their opinions, and yet have no religion at all. And on the other hand persons may be truly religious who hold many wrong opinions."[10] Notice that he says "many" erroneous opinions; he does not say that the truly religious may be wrong in *all* their opinions. He elaborates a few paragraphs

9. Wesley, "The Way to the Kingdom," in Outler, *Sermons*, 1:220-21.
10. Wesley, "On the Trinity," in Outler, *Sermons*, 2:374.

onward: "[W]e cannot but infer that there are ten thousand mistakes which may consist with real religion; with regard to which every candid, considerate man will think and let think. But there are some truths more important than others. It seems there are some which are of deep importance . . . some which it nearly concerns us to know, as having a close connection with vital religion."[11]

What we appear to have here is something quite close to a "grammatical" understanding of doctrine. Knowing the content of Christian doctrinal propositions is one thing; knowing God, or having "a heart right toward God and man,"[12] is another. A person may have a fine grasp of the first, and be nowhere near the second. But the propositions are not pointless: rightly used, they can be instrumental to the knowledge of God. They represent, and guide, proper Christian usage. It is not the propositions as such, but the lived understanding or competence they represent, that is of main importance.

If we think of this lived understanding in the Christian community as the doctrinal substance, and an individual Christian's more or less explicit grasp of it as "opinion," this would seem to correspond roughly to one of Wesley's ways of distinguishing occasionally between "doctrine" and "opinion": "doctrine" is the grammar of the church's language,

---

11. Ibid., 2:376.

12. Wesley, "The Way to the Kingdom," in Outler, *Sermons*, 1:223. Wesley has several characteristic ways of describing "true religion": e.g., "true religion, in the very essence of it, is nothing short of *holy tempers*" ("On Charity," in Outler, *Sermons*, 3:306); "love of God and man" ("On Zeal," in Outler, *Sermons*, 3:313); or "the knowledge and love of God" ("Spiritual Worship," in Outler, *Sermons*, 3:99). These more or less imply one another, given Wesley's understanding of the key concepts involved.

while "opinion" is the individual Christian's conscious understanding of that grammar. If, alternatively, we think of the more essential or vital Christian doctrines as "doctrines," and the less important ones as "opinions," this would represent another, though even less common, occasional Wesleyan usage. (Wesley himself is responsible for a certain amount of the difficulty his interpreters have on this score.)[13]

However it is to be stated, Wesley did recognize a distinction between more and less important doctrines. Even when it came to the more important ones, however, Wesley was reluctant to claim that an *explicit* knowledge of them was essential. There is danger in explication: danger that we will place too much emphasis on having it all worked out the right way, at the expense of vital religion. With the ancient church, he was inclined to think of these most important doctrines more as ones that cannot be safely *denied* than as ones that must be consciously *affirmed*. Denial, for him, seems to imply a conscious rejection of a vital grammatical principle, a decision not to honor it in one's Christian understanding—and in the case of the more important principles, that decision has seriously disruptive effects.[14]

It is commonly observed that John Wesley did not have much to say about the Trinity. It is also commonly observed that Wesley "thinks constantly in Trinitarian terms"[15]; his thought and speech, like the hymnody of his brother Charles, are suffused with usages of the triune name of God and with the understanding that the one God with whom we have to

13. See Maddox, "Opinion, Religion, and 'Catholic Spirit,'" esp. 64–65.

14. See Wesley, "On the Trinity," in Outler, *Sermons*, 2:385–86.

15. Pillow, "John Wesley's Doctrine of the Trinity," 1.

do is "Father, Son, and Holy Ghost." He found explications of the doctrine highly problematic. At the same time, he considered the doctrine of the Trinity (at least in the bare-bones version of it he finds in the first epistle of John: "the Father, the Word, and the Holy Ghost . . . are one"[16]) among those "more important truths" which it "nearly concerns us to know."[17] He avoids any claim that it is "fundamental," because of his reservations about lists of "fundamentals"; but there is no doubt of the seriousness with which he takes it.

According to John Deschner, the doctrine of the Trinity belongs to Wesley's "presupposed theology": as such, it informs both the "articulated theology" of his preaching and writing and the "enacted theology" of his leadership of the Methodist movement, but it is rarely the object of direct and explicit attention.[18] Wesley's relative silence on this doctrine has also been attributed (perhaps dismissively) to his pietism, that is, to a conviction that "abstruse doctrines are better believed devoutly than analysed rationally,"[19] and to a practical decision on his part in that he consistently followed his mother's early advice to him about preaching: "be very cautious of giving definitions in public assemblies, for it does not answer the true end of preaching, which is to mend men's lives, not to fill their heads with unprofitable speculations."[20]

16. 1 John 5:7 (KJV).

17. Wesley, "On the Trinity," in Outler, *Sermons*, 2:376.

18. Deschner, *Wesley's Christology*, xii–xiii.

19. From Outler's introductory comment on Wesley's sermon, "On the Trinity," in Outler, *Sermons*, 1:373.

20. Letter from Susanna Wesley to John Wesley, May 14, 1727, in Baker, *Letters I*, 217. I am indebted to Richard Paul Heitzenrater for this reference from his dissertation, *John Wesley and the Oxford Methodists*, 380–81.

These are not mutually exclusive explanations, and each bears some truth, but they may not yet do full justice to Wesley's way of being trinitarian—neither to the reasons for his reticence about the doctrine, nor to its unique importance in his thought and practice. These matters are worth some further exploration.

Wesley's one published sermon devoted to the subject of the Trinity was evidently an exercise of duty,[21] and a considerable portion of it is spent explaining why talking about the Trinity is a bad idea. It is a bad idea because those who attempt it have a difficult time restricting their talk to an acknowledgement of the *fact* of God's triune reality, but find themselves veering into talk about the *manner* of that reality. *That* "the Father, the Word, and the Holy Ghost" are one is an important truth, revealed to us for our benefit. "It enters into the very heart of Christianity; it lies at the root of all vital religion." *How* they are one has not been revealed. It therefore does not concern us to know this; indeed, it is a mystery beyond our understanding.[22] Wesley endorsed the sweeping judgment of Jonathan Swift that all who have tried to explicate this doctrine have done more harm than good: they "have utterly lost their way; have above all other persons hurt the cause which they intended to promote, having only, as Job speaks, 'darkened counsel by words without knowledge.'"[23]

Although Wesley's (and Swift's) negative judgment on this enterprise was not limited to any particular period, his own seems to have been a particularly inauspicious age for explications of trinitarian doctrine. Since the late seventeenth

21. Klaiber and Marquardt, *Gelebte Gnade*, 50–51.
22. Wesley, "On the Trinity," in Outler, *Sermons*, 2:384.
23. Ibid., 1:377.

century, British treatises on the Trinity had been notorious for falling into heresy, either deliberately or inadvertently, largely through their efforts to rationalize what Wesley would call the "manner" of God's being three-in-one in a way that would meet newly-emerging criteria of intelligibility. William Sherlock's well-meaning "vindication" of the doctrine of the Trinity against contemporary Socinian attacks, published in 1690, is a stock example of the problem: it seems to have backfired in just the way Wesley describes. The *Dictionary of National Biography* wryly notes: "If the Socinians gained any advantage in the controversy, it was from Sherlock they got it. . . . This book had the singular effect of making a Socinian of William Manning [a congregational minister who became an influential advocate of Socinian views after reading Sherlock] and an Arian of Thomas Emlyn [a presbyterian whom the *DNB* identifies as the first unitarian minister in England]."[24] As the influence of Locke and Newton grew, it became more and more difficult to make any sense of the Trinity—or to give any room to it in one's mental universe.[25] Wesley's favorable attitude toward William Jones's *The Catholic Doctrine of a Trinity* (first published in 1754) is surely related to the fact that Jones avoids any explanation of the "how" of the Trinity, and simply gathers together the biblical texts that (as traditionally construed and connected) prove the divinity, the distinctions, and the unity of the three persons of the Godhead.

24. "Sherlock, William," in *Dictionary of National Biography*, 18:96.

25. A lucid older account of this is Cragg, *From Puritanism to the Age of Reason*, esp. 101–4. Buckley, *At the Origins of Modern Atheism*, is a brilliant treatment of the broader European picture. On the doctrine of the Trinity in England in particular, see Babcock, "A Changing of the Christian God: The Doctrine of the Trinity in the Seventeenth Century."

Jones is content, that is, to state the fact, and not to inquire into the manner, of God's three-in-oneness.[26]

Merely stating the fact of the Trinity in scriptural terms may avoid the dangers Wesley saw in more reasoned explications of the doctrine, but it may also fail (as Wesley admits it did in Jones's case) to give much indication of what that fact has to do with human and Christian life.[27] It does not yet show how, as Wesley claims, "[t]he knowledge of the Three-One God is interwoven with all true Christian faith, with all vital religion."[28] How is this claim justified?

Note his language here: "the knowledge of the Three-One God." It is not the mere knowledge *that* God is triune, but knowledge *of* the triune God, that Wesley finds at the heart of Christian faith. What does it mean to know the "Three-One God"?

---

26. "The Scripture is the only rule that can enable us to judge, whether [Arianism] or the Catholic Doctrine of the Trinity is more agreeable to truth; therefore I have confined myself to this unexceptionable kind of evidence for the proof of the latter, and have made the Scripture *its own interpreter*." Jones, preface to the 2nd edition (1767) of *The Catholic Doctrine of a Trinity*, viii–ix. Various Methodist scholars (e.g., Lycurgus M. Starkey Jr., Geoffrey Wainwright, and Randy Maddox) have called attention to Wesley's commendation of the book in his letter of April 17, 1776 to Mary Bishop, and I am indebted to them for this reference. See Telford, *Letters of the Rev. John Wesley*, 6:213–14.

27. "Mr. Jones's book on the Trinity is both more clear and more strong than any I ever saw on that subject. If anything is wanting, it is the application, lest it should appear to be a merely speculative doctrine, which has no influence on our hearts or lives; but this is abundantly supplied by my brother's *Hymns*." Telford, *Letters*, 6:213.

28. Wesley, "On the Trinity," in Outler, *Sermons*, 1:385.

In his 1780 sermon on "Spiritual Worship," Wesley characterizes the Christian religion as the happy and loving knowledge of the true God:

> [F]or as none is now, so none was ever happy without the loving knowledge of the true God.... [T]his happy knowledge of the true God is only another name for *religion*; I mean *Christian* religion, which indeed is the only one that deserves the name. Religion, as to the nature or essence of it, does not lie in this or that set of notions, vulgarly called "faith"; nor in a round of duties, however carefully "reformed" from error and superstition. It does not consist in any number of outward actions. No; it properly and directly consists in the knowledge and love of God, as manifested in the Son of his love, through the eternal Spirit. And this naturally leads to every heavenly temper, and to every good word and work.[29]

Note the qualifying expressions: this is "*happy* knowledge," it is "*loving* knowledge," and it is knowledge of "the *true* God." It is not just happenstance that Wesley chooses these three qualifiers for the knowledge of God Christians are given to share. The knowledge of God is for Wesley a participation in the life of God (religion is "the union of the soul with God, the life of God in the soul of man"[30]), and that means a participation in God's truth, in God's love, and in God's happiness. The knowledge of the triune God is, we might say, a triune knowledge.

29. Wesley, "Spiritual Worship," in Outler, *Sermons*, 3:99.
30. Wesley, "Upon Our Lord's Sermon on the Mount, Discourse the Fourth," in Outler, *Sermons*, 1:541.

This threefold pattern occurs repeatedly in Wesley's references to the human vocation—that is, to what human life is for, what we are meant to do and to become as human creatures. To be created in the image of God, he says in a sermon published in 1782, is to be "designed to know, to love, and to enjoy [our] Creator to all eternity."[31] The image of God was the theme of the first sermon Wesley preached at Oxford, in 1730, and there, in somewhat different terminology, the same three features occur, supplemented by freedom as a fourth. The image of God, as exhibited in our first parents, consists first in an understanding that is "just," "swift," "clear," and "great"; second, in "rational, even, and regular" affections ("if we may be allowed to say 'affections,' for properly speaking he had but one: man was what God is, Love"); third, in liberty, a "perfect freedom implanted in [human] nature and interwoven with all its parts"; and fourth, in happiness ("Then to live was to enjoy").[32] If we understand freedom as a sort of transcendental feature, a condition of the possibility of understanding and love and happiness, "interwoven" (as Wesley says) with all the rest, this fourfold explication might be harmonized with the more common threefold one.[33] Clearly, each of these three capacities can only be exercised in freedom, just as each of them is a *relational* capacity. Understanding, love, and delight are all "transitive," that is, each has an object. Indeed, in the theological context, each is supremely relational, in that our relationship to God is also a relationship to everything else

---

31. Wesley, "God's Approbation of His Works," in Outler, *Sermons*, 2:397.

32. Wesley, "The Image of God," in Outler, *Sermons*, 4:293–95.

33. Cf. Jürgen Moltmann's interweaving of freedom with the not-dissimilar triad of faith, love, and hope, in *Der Geist des Lebens*, 127–33.

that is. Knowing God, loving God, rejoicing in or giving thanks to God—each capacity is exercised in responsive (and responsible) relationship with God and creation.[34]

These characteristics emerge clearly in Wesley's handling of the metaphor of God's "light" in this connection. In a comment on John 1:4b, "and the life was the light of men," in his *Explanatory Notes Upon the New Testament*, he says: "He who is essential life, and the Giver of life to all that liveth, was also the light of men, the fountain of wisdom, holiness, and happiness to man in his original state."[35] The metaphor receives more extensive treatment in his sermon on Matthew 6:19–23 in the series on the Sermon on the Mount. "The light of the body is the eye: if therefore thine eye be single [i.e., healthy], thy whole body shall be full of light," runs Matthew 6:22. According to Wesley, the "light" which fills a person whose eye is "single" consists first in "true, divine knowledge," "wisdom," "understanding"; second, in "holiness," "the light of the glorious love of God," "the love of God and man"; and third, in "happiness," "comfort," "peace," "rejoicing," "rejoicing evermore, praying without ceasing, and in everything giving thanks, *enjoying* whatever is the will of God concerning [one]

---

34. Wesley perpetuates what is to my mind a deeply unfortunate tendency to speak disjunctively about our relationship to God and creation. In "The Image of God," our first parents' choice was "to enjoy either the Creator or the creation" (Outler, *Sermons*, 4:295); in "Spiritual Idolatry," this either/or is pursued relentlessly (Outler, *Sermons*, 3:103–14). The intention may have been to warn against *inordinate* relations to the creation, and perhaps we are to understand that—as Wesley makes quite clear in other places—love to God includes or implies a proper love toward God's creatures; but the disjunctive rhetoric Wesley inherited and used suggests otherwise, and has had unfortunate (if unintended) effects.

35. Wesley, *Explanatory Notes*, 303.

in Christ Jesus."[36] These are all relational realities, created and sustained by the inflowing light of God, and directed back to God. They also involve our freedom. We know freedom in the light of God, and exercise that freedom in the fulfillment of our vocation to know, love, and rejoice in God. We may also use (and forsake) that freedom in turning from the light; and when that happens, knowledge, holiness, and happiness are replaced by their opposites: "ignorance and error" in place of understanding, "ungodliness and unrighteousness" (i.e., evil affections) in place of the holiness of love, and "misery" ("destruction and unhappiness") in place of joy.[37]

In his whole treatment of this theme of our "chief end" as human beings, there is very little explicit indication of a correlation between the three facets of our vocation and the three "persons" of the Trinity. Wesley does not give us a developed doctrine of the *imago Dei* as an *imago Trinitatis*, for instance.[38] Suggestions of a correlation between the threefold pattern of our vocation and the triunity of God only emerge as he moves to talk about our recovery of the image of God, our restoration to our vocation to understanding, love, and

---

36. Wesley, "Upon our Lord's Sermon on the Mount," in Outler, *Sermons*, 1:613–15.

37. Ibid., 1:615–16. In "The Image of God," the same sad story is told in connection with the Fall: the understanding was slowed and confused; the will, having lost the guidance of the understanding, was "seized by legions of vile affections"; "liberty went away with virtue" so the human creature was captive to those vile affections; and happiness was gone, misery arrived. Wesley, "The Image of God," in Outler, *Sermons*, 4:298–99.

38. His contemporary, Jonathan Edwards, whose language manifests a strikingly similar trinitarian grammar, does so, as do Augustine and the Cappadocians in their own ways.

thanksgiving—in other words, about salvation, the heart of his "articulated theology."

Wesley knew and honored the ancient principle that *opera Trinitatis ad extra indivisa sunt*: everything that God does "outwardly," that is, with regard to creatures, is to be ascribed to the entire Trinity, and we are not to ascribe any such act of God to any one of the trinitarian persons exclusively. If we speak, for instance, of sanctification as the work of the Holy Spirit, this is not to be understood as excluding the involvement of the other two persons in sanctification, but instead is a way of calling attention to a particular relationship between what is distinctive about this "person" of the Trinity (as we understand these distinctions on the basis of scripture) and this particular divine work. The technical name for this kind of association between a particular person of the Trinity and a particular work of the entire Trinity is "appropriation." Wesley regularly and deliberately practiced this manner of speaking, not least in his language about salvation. He will, for example, readily "appropriate" justification to the Son and sanctification to the Spirit, or utilize a general narrative scheme summarized by Geoffrey Wainwright thus: "The Father saw the human need for salvation, the Son supplied it, the Holy Spirit applies it."[39]

However, Wesley's way of correlating "persons" of the Trinity and aspects of God's working goes beyond this. A hint of what more is involved comes early in his discussion of salvation in the 1765 sermon, "The Scripture Way of Salvation." Salvation begins with "preventing grace," and Wesley's description of that phenomenon in a single lengthy sentence gives it a striking trinitarian shape: Preventing grace is "all the

---

39. Wainwright, "Why Wesley Was a Trinitarian," 40.

'drawings' of 'the Father', the desires after God, which, if we yield to them, increase more and more; all that 'light' wherewith the Son of God 'enlighteneth everyone that cometh into the world', *showing* every man 'to do justly, to love mercy, and to walk humbly with his God'; all the *convictions* which his Spirit from time to time works in every child of man."[40] There is here, we might say, a foretaste of happiness, a yearning for God, associated with the "Father"; an incipient knowledge of God, in which the "Son" somehow figures; and the first stirring of the will and affections toward the possibility of newness of life, attributed to the "Spirit"—all in connection with prevenient grace. The correlations are made more explicit and extensive in a brief description of the dynamics of salvation in a later sermon:

> This eternal life then commences when it pleases the Father to reveal his Son in our hearts; when we first know Christ, being enabled to "call him Lord by the Holy Ghost"; when we can testify, our conscience bearing us witness in the Holy Ghost, "the life which I now live, I live by faith in the Son of God, who loved me, and gave himself for me." And then it is that happiness begins—happiness real, solid, substantial. Then it is that heaven is opened in the soul, that the proper, heavenly state commences, while the love of God, as loving us, is shed abroad in the heart, instantly producing love to all mankind: general, pure benevolence, together with its genuine fruits, lowliness, meekness, patience, contentedness in every state; an entire, clear, full acquiescence in the whole will of God, enabling

---

40. John Wesley, "The Scripture Way of Salvation," in Outler, *Sermons*, 2:156–57.

us to "rejoice evermore, and in everything to give thanks."[41]

What is going on in these accounts of God's working is more than a matter of "appropriations." Note, in the quotation just given, that all three "persons" are involved, *distinctively*, in our coming to the knowledge of God: the "Father" reveals the "Son" (at the same time, and in another sense, the "Son" can be said to reveal the "Father"), and this knowledge is received and appropriated "in the Spirit." The one event of our knowing has its source in the "Father," its substance in the "Son," and its realization in the "Spirit." We are brought to participate in God's own knowledge of God's self. This knowledge is the ground of our happiness, for it is the knowledge of the love of God for us, restoring us to life as we come to delight in God. We are brought to share in God's own joy. At the same time, God's love toward us becomes God's love working in us as it is "shed abroad in the heart" and becomes our love toward all that God loves. We are brought to participate in the love of God. There is, so to speak, a mutual indwelling of our understanding, love, and happiness, which is itself a mirroring of the divine *perichoresis*, the participation of the persons of the Trinity in one another. Geoffrey Wainwright makes the point well: "In sum, our salvation is for Wesley the differentiated but united work of the Three Persons of the Godhead; it sets us into an appropriate relation to each Person, and it gives us . . . a share in their divine communion. The Holy Trinity appears, therefore, as both the origin and goal of soteriology."[42] We are made for this trinitarian communion; our rejection

---

41. John Wesley, "Spiritual Worship," in Outler, *Sermons*, 3:96.
42. Wainwright, "Why Wesley Was a Trinitarian," 35.

of this vocation has its own dismal threefold shape; and our restoration to it by the grace of the Three-One God takes it to a new level of meaning.

This way of understanding the triune pattern of God's action and the triune character of our human destiny came to both John and Charles Wesley, I suppose, as they took in (or were taken into) the "depth grammar" of the biblical canon. Of course, they were taught that grammar not by "scripture alone" but by a community (or set of communities) of speakers of this Christian language, including their parents, their contemporaries, the authors of the Book of Common Prayer and other shapers of the discourse of their church, and the framers and interpreters of early catholic Christian doctrine. In John's case at least, the influence of early Eastern Christianity upon his grasp and articulation of the key trinitarian pattern may have been substantial. But the pattern itself is pervasive. It is only illustrative of its power that when, in "Love Divine, All Loves Excelling," Charles describes what it will mean to see the face of God, it comes out as being "lost in wonder, love, and praise."

How might this exploration inform our understanding of doctrine in the Methodist traditions? Its chief contribution might be in its illuminating the *instrumental* character of doctrinal statements. To help in considering this, let us call to mind a threefold distinction in the meaning of "doctrine." What we might call "objective doctrine," that is, doctrinal statements and formulations (similar to grammatical principles and paradigms), can be distinguished from what we might call "subjective doctrine," that is, the conceptual substance of the lived understanding of the faith (similar to the actual grammatical structure of a language as it is used by competent speakers), and both can be distinguished from what we might call "active doctrine," that is, the teaching activity in which, usually by means of doctrinal statements of one sort or another, doctrinal competence is fostered. Ordinarily, when we hear the word "doctrine" we think of doctrinal statements (objective doctrine). An appreciation of the other senses of the term may assist us in understanding what those doctrinal statements are actually for: they are points of reference whereby we may measure, in some respects, the adequacy of our attempts to communicate the Christian faith, and they are guides to Christian understanding. They have their role, then, in those activities of teaching and reflection in which the conceptual capacities sustaining the knowledge and love of God are developed and strengthened. A key test of their own adequacy is their effectiveness in those activities.

The report of a recent study commission of the British Council of Churches reflects an understanding of the role of doctrine, and of the doctrine of the Trinity in particular, that seems quite consonant with the Wesleyan insights we have been exploring, when in its conclusion it observes that "the difference between the life and death of Christian worship depends upon its recovery of a trinitarian dynamic," and then goes on to say: "Our concern is not that trinitarian words and phrases should be incorporated in liturgies and hymns in a merely cosmetic way, but that worshippers should celebrate and be drawn into the life and relationships of the triune God."[43] We might well learn some things from John Wesley's own doctrinal practice to help the churches toward this goal.

---

43. British Council of Churches, *Report of the BCC Study Commission*, 28.

2

WESLEYAN CONSTRUCTIVE THEOLOGY

THE VARIETY OF adjectives which may be found preceding the noun "theology" can be confusing. There is Jewish theology and Christian theology, natural, historical, and dogmatic theology, biblical, liberal, feminist, and evangelical theology—the list could be extended into the dozens. These adjectives do not all perform the same service: some indicate an approach, some delimit the subject-matter, and others declare a particular commitment or concern. It is not always easy to tell just what is being indicated, or how the adjective qualifies the noun and the enterprise.

Few of these terms have escaped censure of one kind or another. Those who view revelation as the ground of theology may declare natural theology impossible. Systematic theology may appear overweening to those struck by the mystery and freedom of God. So-called liberal and evangelical theologies alike may seem to be question-begging efforts, in which the theologian's allegiance to a particular point of view compromises the inquiry from the start. Dogmatic theology may connote a narrow preoccupation with right beliefs and their formulation. Nearly every sort of theology which an adjective may suggest has been called into question, with more or less justice. The bare noun, "theology," is, of course, intolerably uninformative, and anyone who intends to forswear adjectives and to study, teach, or practice just plain theology should be prepared for a reaction of skepticism or impatience from those to whom that intention is announced. But although the adjectives may be practically unavoidable, the problematic character of most of the resulting terms indicates the importance of giving careful consideration to their choice and use.

"Wesleyan constructive theology," the theme of the working group of Methodist theologians at which the following reflections were first presented, is, naturally enough, doubly suspect. It would be well for us to clarify the sense in which a theological endeavor might properly be "constructive" and "Wesleyan." My aim here is to propose such a clarification. Of course, one may fairly ask whether it is worthwhile to use the phrase or to pursue the enterprise thus designated at all. This essay will not answer this question, though it may contribute in some way to an answer.

I.

Whether Christian theology ought to be constructive at all is a debated issue. To some, the task of theology is essentially analytical and descriptive: it is to identify and unfold the truths already received in the sources of the church's tradition. On this view, theological construction amounts to infidelity. To do "constructive theology" would be to prefer the product of one's own imagination to "the faith once delivered to the saints." To the extent that it is faithful to its task, theology avoids construction. To others, however, theology is essentially constructive; it is, to use a phrase prominent in the recent work of Gordon Kaufman, "imaginative construction," and the more fully this is acknowledged, the more adequate the construction is likely to be. To ignore or deny the constructive character of theology is to delude oneself. There can be no simply descriptive theology.

The force of this latter claim, against any naive and ahistorical attempt simply to recover and transmit the primitive, uninterpreted gospel, can readily be felt. We know that perception is already interpretation, that any theologian's description of the faith is influenced in countless ways by his or her circumstances, and that therefore theology will always in some sense be a constructive endeavor, whether intentionally so or not. And it makes sense, granting all this, to be candid and self-aware about this necessity. Theology, like all works of the human mind, is inevitably constructive.

But if all theology is constructive, what might be meant by the phrase, "constructive theology"? If it is not simply pleonasm, this phrase must designate a particular type or aspect of theology, distinguishing it from other types or aspects (however "constructive," in the first sense, they may also be). How might this be understood? At what point must Christian theology be particularly constructive, and what is the nature of this construction? To gain some clarity about this, it may be helpful to envision the task of Christian theology as a whole.

Christian theology may be defined as a critical inquiry into the validity of Christian witness.[1] That inquiry has three

1. For a fuller treatment of the following scheme, see Wood, *Vision and Discernment*, chap. 3.

basic dimensions, each corresponding to an essential formal feature of the concept of "Christian witness." First, because Christian witness always conveys an implicit or explicit claim to be Christian, there is the fundamental question of its Christianness: Is this act of witness—past, present, or envisioned—truly Christian? Secondly, because Christian witness also conveys a claim to truth, there is the fundamental question of its truth: Is this really true? Thirdly, because Christian witness is an act of communication and not a performance in a vacuum, there is the fundamental question of its aptness as communication: Is this act of witness fitting to its context and to its purpose in that context? Is the Christian witness validly enacted here?

To each of these three fundamental questions there corresponds a principal theological discipline. We may, for convenience, call these disciplines by the familiar titles of historical theology, philosophical theology, and practical theology, respectively, though the titles are negotiable and relatively unimportant. Historical theology, on this usage, is not simply the historical study of the Christian tradition. It is a theological discipline which uses historical inquiry to pursue the critical question of the Christianness of Christian witness. It reflects upon the way the church has always appealed to elements of its own tradition to vindicate the Christian authenticity of its life and message, and it asks two main questions about this process: First, what is it in the past which may most adequately serve as the criterion or criteria for testing the representativeness of Christian witness, i.e., its faithfulness to Jesus Christ about whom it claims to be? (What, in other words, is the "canon" by which the church's representation of Jesus Christ may be measured?) And secondly, when may

Wesleyan Constructive Theology 27

an instance of witness rightly be said to be "in accord" with the criterion or criteria thus identified? What does it mean to be faithful? Historical theology investigates the Christian tradition so as to inform and enhance contemporary reflection upon the problems of the identity, continuity, unity, and representativeness of Christian witness, in its manifold and ever-increasing variety.

Philosophical theology—understood here as a discipline of Christian theology, not as a synonym for "natural theology" or "philosophy of religion"—uses the resources of philosophical reflection to pursue the question of the truth of Christian witness. It aims to discover and display the logic of Christian witness, i.e., the principles governing its meaning, so as to clarify the sorts of claims it makes, and then to see what may be said about the truth of those claims.

Practical theology studies the practice of Christian witness, with particular attention not to its origin (historical theology) nor to its nature (philosophical theology) but to its goal, its intention. It asks by what standards the practice of Christian witness ought to be judged in the light of its goal, and it proceeds to make the relevant judgments concerning a given instance of witness, past, present, or prospective. Because Christian witness is itself a matter of human conduct, and because it always takes place within a particular human situation, practical theology draws upon the various disciplines concerned with human behavior (e.g., sociology, anthropology, and psychology) as resources for its inquiry. It studies the ways in which society and culture shape Christian witness and influence its reception; but it goes beyond a description of this process, to make critical judgments regarding the adequacy of Christian practice, and to ask the normative question of how witness may be most fittingly enacted within a given set of circumstances.

Three principal theological disciplines thus take shape around the three fundamental critical questions which are to be raised about the validity of Christian witness as such. Put in positive form, the questions are: What is truly Christian witness? What is the truth of Christian witness? How is Christian witness fittingly enacted? Although these are distinct questions, none of them may be pursued in isolation from the others. It is, for example, impossible to fully determine the meaning and truth of an utterance apart from a consideration of its origin and its intention in a particular context. It is impossible to assess the fitness of a given act of witness, or even to identify the pertinent criteria for such an assessment, without attending to the nature of Christian witness as such, as well as to the variety of its historical expressions. And it is impossible to locate the criteria of Christian authenticity in the Christian tradition if one is unprepared to read the tradition as the history of Christian practice, i.e., to bring the resources of practical theological reflection to bear upon historical theology. These three inquiries are interdependent in many ways. That interdependence is also a feature of the cognate secular disciplines which correspond to these three dimensions of theology: neither "history" nor "philosophy" nor "the human sciences" names a single discipline with a single identifiable method; all three are large and unruly fields of inquiry, interconnecting and overlapping in various interesting ways.

Those familiar with the so-called "Wesleyan quadrilateral" of scripture, tradition, experience, and reason as theological guidelines may recognize a parallel between those guidelines and their interaction, on the one hand, and the foregoing sketch of the three basic lines of theological inquiry and their interaction, on the other. At the considerable risk of oversimplification, let us see whether the parallel may be made more precise and explicit. "Scripture," "reason," and "experience," the shorthand labels of three members of the quartet, may be correlated fairly clearly with the inquiries here labeled (respectively) historical, philosophical, and practical theology. To test whether a given utterance or action is "scriptural" is to test its Christian authenticity, that is, its capacity to represent the Christ to whom scripture bears definitive witness—assuming, of course, as Wesley certainly did, that it is "scripture" and not something else which performs that function, and assuming that one has an appropriate way of understanding and applying scripture so as to be able to determine when something is in accord with it. (For Wesley, "tradition" had something substantial to do with this question of how one reads and uses scripture; but then, so did "experience" and "reason." Given the primacy of scripture for him, it seems best to associate this dimension of theological inquiry with "scripture" simply, and not with "scripture and tradition"—though a case could also be made for the latter alternative.) The discipline of historical theology does not, of course, simply assume that "scripture" has this role, since that is one of the things about which it has to inquire; but the underlying question as to the Christian authenticity of what the church says and does is the same.

"Reason," in the language of this approach to theological accountability, represents the question of the meaning and truth of Christian witness—the question of what is here called "philosophical theology." In Wesley's own understanding, the gospel is not only to be commended as true and believed to be true, it is to be apprehended as true. It is not only reasonable in the sense that it accords with the eternal Logos, it is also reasonable in the sense that human reason—once in possession of the evidence of faith—can understand and affirm it through ordinary processes of inference and judgment.[2] "Scripture and reason" are both to be consulted in the testing of Christian utterance. Or, to put it another way, we are entitled and obliged to satisfy ourselves as to the truth as well as the "scripturality" of what is presented as Christian witness before we affirm it for ourselves or proffer it to others. Indeed, apart from some exercise of reason along these lines, it is doubtful that we can be said even to understand it.

The category of "experience" may be correlated with the concern of practical theology: How may Christian witness be so enacted as to achieve its proper goal? Valid witness is known by its fruit, i.e., by its capacity to transform personal and social existence in appropriate ways. A particular representation of the gospel will attest itself—or fail to do so—in the way it influences the lives of the persons and the society to which it is addressed. A form of witness which is suited to one situation may be ineffective, or negative in its effects, in another, and so practical theology must always be contextually specific as it works out the relationship between witness and experience.

"Scripture," "reason," and "experience" thus represent, in Wesleyan language, the three major tests to which Christian witness—"tradition," to use the fourth term of the quartet—is subjected in theological reflection. "Tradition" and "witness"

2. Wesley, *An Earnest Appeal to Men of Reason and Religion*, in Cragg, *Appeals to Men*, 55–57.

are functionally equivalent terms in this connection. Both can refer to the process as well as to the content, to the activity of "bearing" or "handing on" as well as to that which is borne or handed on. Tradition or witness is also that which, in a sense, bears us: comprehensively understood, it is the ongoing Christian movement through which we have our own Christian existence. Tradition, so understood, is less an external reference-point we consult than it is the environment in which we find ourselves, and with whose care we are entrusted.

Christian theology is critical reflection upon Christian tradition: both upon the tradition which has been inherited and upon the "traditioning" yet to be done. It subjects that tradition to a threefold test. We have seen that each of the three principal lines of theological inquiry is dependent upon the other two. We have also seen that the critical question central to each is also capable of positive or constructive formulation. Since critical inquiry presupposes criteria, some attempt to answer these positive questions (What makes Christian witness Christian? What does it mean to claim that it is the truth? How might its fitting enactment be described?) is requisite to the critical task as such.

The pursuit of these positive questions as to the authenticity, truth, and fitting enactment of Christian witness drives these three inquiries into close interaction, indeed, into a unified pattern of reflection.[3] A fourth principal theological discipline thus emerges at the point of intersection of the first three. "Systematic theology," to use the conventional term, is

3. There are, of course, a number of contrary forces to be reckoned with, as many recent writings on the reform of theological studies have pointed out.

constituted by the effort to bring the three basic theological inquiries together in a comprehensive and constructive fashion. It is "systematic" in three senses: First, it integrates the three basic inquiries, bringing the resources and insights of each to bear upon each of the others, and striving for coherence. Secondly, it is comprehensive in its scope: it attempts to deal with the whole of the Christian witness, giving attention to its consistency and integrity. And thirdly, it is indeed *constructive* theology: it attempts to offer a positive answer to the question of what constitutes valid (authentic, true, and fitting) Christian witness, for a given situation or range of situations. The answer thus reached may find written expression in what is frequently called "a systematic theology," that is, a comprehensive statement of the Christian faith according to some explicit principles of interpretation and organization. But it need not. Occasional essays addressed to particular issues in the primary disciplines of historical, philosophical, and practical theology, focused treatments of specific doctrines or aspects of witness, and many other sorts of published work may manifest the results of systematic theological reflection, as may—and should—the "enacted theology"[4] of actual Christian practice: church polity, corporate worship, social witness, and the rest. "Systematic theology" in the strict sense properly designates a mode of theological reflection, and is applied only derivatively to its results. And we might well be wary of associating the term exclusively with one sort

---

4. John Deschner refers to Wesley's "articulated theology," "presuppositional theology," and "enacted theology" as three distinct resources to be taken into account in any attempt to take his theological measure. It is a distinction with wider possibilities. See Deschner, *Wesley's Christology*, xii–xiii.

of literature, especially when what may be called for in a given situation is a quite different way of bringing out the results of systematic reflection.

"Constructive theology," then, may be taken to designate this positive aspect of systematic theology, and, by extension, its working out into the various sorts of theological proposals which the exigencies and opportunities of Christian witness may seem to call for.

II.

But what might Wesleyan constructive theology be? It would appear that the term, "Wesleyan theology," might be taken in at least two distinct senses—leaving aside its casual use to designate either Wesley's own theology or the theology produced by persons in the Wesleyan tradition, however defined. In one sense, "Wesleyan" refers to a theological criterion; in the other, it refers to the subject-matter receiving our theological attention. That is, "Wesleyan theology" might refer to an effort to identify that which is authentically Wesleyan, and to evaluate church doctrine and practice in the light of that standard. Alternatively, it might refer to the effort to subject the Wesleyan tradition itself to critical scrutiny—to test its adequacy as Christian witness.

Both sorts of Wesleyan theology have been pursued with more or less vigor in the past two hundred years, and both have their uses. At first glance, the former sort would appear useful to the church's concern—such as it is—for doctrinal discipline, by helping the church to identify, understand, and apply the standards of doctrine to which it is committed. It is, however, instructive that the "normative Wesleyanism" of, e.g., the United Methodist doctrinal standards understands itself to be somewhat less than normative: it appeals constantly to the criterion of scripture,[5] takes responsibility for its own place within the broader Christian tradition, and holds itself open to the tests of reason and experience. A Wesleyan theology in this first sense which takes this fact seriously, rather than elevating Wesley's utterances as a material norm, is on the way to becoming a Wesleyan theology in the second sense: that is, a critical examination of the validity of the Wesleyan movement and message as Christian witness.

It is to this sort of Wesleyan theology that John Wesley himself exhorted his readers.[6] And if "constructive theology" refers to that aspect of the whole theological task which generates new possibilities for the understanding and furtherance of Christian witness, perhaps "Wesleyan constructive theology" is best understood simply as the sort of constructive theology which emerges out of such critical engagement with the Wesleyan heritage.

---

5. Cf. Article V of the Articles of Religion, and the prefaces and contents of Wesley's *Standard Sermons* and *Notes on the New Testament*.

6. The three questions traditionally asked of those seeking admission into full connection in a United Methodist annual conference enforce this exhortation: "Have you studied the doctrines of the United Methodist Church? After full examination do you believe that our doctrines are in harmony with the Holy Scriptures? Will you preach and maintain them?"

THE PRIMACY of SCRIPTURE

PEOPLE CAN BE divided into two groups, James Thurber says somewhere: there are those who divide people into two groups, and there are those who don't. I belong to the second group. (That may be a self-falsifying statement, but never mind.) I have the distinct impression that mine is the smaller of the two groups, as the tendency to divide people into two groups seems to spring eternal in the human breast. The tendency is perfectly understandable. In fact, it has so many things going for it that it is a wonder that any of us manage to register even momentary dissent from it—and when we do, that dissent is marked by the delightful irony that Thurber's remark embodies.

Not least among the evident advantages of binary thinking and binary rhetoric, besides the obvious psychological ones, are some political ones. If you are seeking a greater share of influence, it is decidedly helpful to be able to present yourself as representing one of the two serious options, rather than, say, one of five, or one of seventeen. To reduce the options through judicious reinterpretation from some unwieldy number to just two, and to identify yourself with one of them, is not a bad strategy—particularly if you can also make it clear that yours is the only really acceptable option. The process of binary redescription lends itself admirably to that cause. It is an oppositional process at its core, after all. The two groups are not "A" and "B" (a nomenclature that would open up the possibility of "C" and "D" and . . . where would it all end?!); they are "A" and "not-A," and the "not" in "not-A" has to be understood in a fairly strong sense: the groups, or the positions and values they represent, are antithetical.

This way of thinking and speaking need not be overtly oppositional, nor even overtly binary. A popular variation is to divide people into *three* groups—say, "left," "right," and "center"—and to take one's place modestly in the center, as the one whose porridge is neither too hot nor too cold, but just right. "Left" and "right" can then easily be assimilated to each other as representing what the center is not. The center represents moderation, reasonableness, balance. The alternative is extremism, unreasonableness, imbalance. "Claiming the center" is a popular move in American religion just as in American politics, dominated as both are by a dysfunctional two-party system. One party claims the center, portrays the other party as a party of extremists, and, as an added benefit, gets to write off the lunatic fringe of its own party as well, at least as a matter of form.

In a statement issued on March 2, 2000—about a month before the quadrennial United Methodist General Conference—an *ad hoc* group of twenty-eight United Methodist evangelicals called for an end to dialogue in the church. According to the United Methodist New Service release, the spokesperson for the group said that

> the denomination's diversity dialogues in 1997 and 1998 showed that "one group believes Scripture is the decisive revelation of God, and the other side believes there are other revelations that transcend or even trump Scripture. Those are diametrically opposed." Further dialogue would only exacerbate the differences or force both sides to compromise their principles, he said.[1]

Now, whether the diversity dialogues showed what this statement takes them to have shown is a question on which judgments may differ. The official report of the dialogues offers a somewhat more ambiguous picture. It does not divide us quite so neatly into two opposing groups. Its description of our differences implies that those United Methodists who agree that scripture is the decisive revelation of God might still disagree as to what scripture teaches on a given subject, or as to how its teaching is to be brought to bear upon a particular issue such as the moral assessment of homosexual relationships. To be sure, the report also asserts that *some* United Methodists who wish to change the church's current position on this particular issue "believe themselves to be the recipients of new revelation from God that is beyond the canon of scripture." And the rhetoric of the document as a whole creates the impression that those who favor the church's acceptance of homosexual relationships tend to give less weight to scripture while those who oppose such acceptance tend to give more weight to scripture in their deliberations.[2] The spokesperson for the *ad hoc* group may have oversimplified the outcome of the diver-

1. United Methodist News Service, "Evangelicals call for move to higher ground," March 8, 2000.

2. Abraham, "In Search of Unity," sec. III.B.1.

sity dialogues, but he was aided in that oversimplification by the official report itself.

In any case, as you ponder his depiction (as quoted in the news release) of the two groups into which United Methodists can be divided, you may experience a momentary doubt as to its adequacy. Recall that in his portrayal, one group accepts the Bible as the decisive revelation of God, and draws the appropriate conclusions as to what the Bible teaches, while the other group—"the other side," as he puts it tellingly—opts for other revelations. You may have wondered, as I did, whether he wasn't (perhaps inadvertently) leaving a few people out. Are those two really the only options to be found among us?

It appears to me that neither of these two groups would be very happy with the current statement in *The Book of Discipline* on "Doctrinal Standards and Our Theological Task."[3] That fact alone may be sufficient reason to give that statement a second look, for it suggests that the dramatic scenario we have been given here may have very little to do with the actuality of the United Methodist Church.

The current statement was adopted by the General Conference of 1988 as a revision of the original 1972 statement—a revision undertaken to address some points in the original that were causing some difficulty. It is, I think, best seen not as a repudiation but rather as a clarification and refinement of the original, in the light of several years' experience. Three features of the resulting, present statement seem to me especially beneficial. Each of them tends to subvert the pattern of thinking exhibited by those who would divide us into two groups. One is the clear distinction introduced between doc-

3. See "Doctrinal Standards and Our Theological Task," in United Methodist Church, *Book of Discipline* (1988), 50–90.

trine and theology. A second is the fact that distinct functions are assigned to scripture, tradition, experience, and reason in the church's theological reflection. And a third is the affirmation and explanation of the primacy of scripture. I want to say something about each of these points, each of which has to do with our practice as a church.

DOCTRINE AND THEOLOGY

One of the earliest criticisms of the 1972 statement was that it represented "a failure to grasp the difference between the role of doctrinal standards in the church and the task of theology," so that the statement's

> concern for theological freedom entails an obscuring of the proper role of doctrinal standards; while ... its ... concern for doctrinal responsibility entails an obscuring of the theological task. . . . [T]heological freedom and doctrinal responsibility are so understood that they can only be played off against one another, with the result that justice is done to neither—though . . . rather less injustice is done to theological freedom than to doctrinal discipline.[4]

The 1988 statement makes a vital contribution at this point. It introduces a functional distinction between doctrine and theology, and thus between doctrinal standards and theological guidelines. "Our doctrinal affirmations assist us in the discernment of Christian truth in ever-changing contexts. Our theological task includes the testing, renewal, elaboration, and application of our doctrinal perspective . . . ."[5] The

---

4. Ogden, "Doctrinal Standards in the United Methodist Church," 42.
5. United Methodist Church, *Book of Discipline* (1988), 77–78.

church's doctrinal standards are the Articles of Religion and the Confession of Faith, as constitutionally-protected *de jure* standards, and Wesley's Standard Sermons and *Explanatory Notes upon the New Testament*, operating *de facto* as shapers of our doctrinal identity. The theological guidelines the church commends are the familiar four elements of the so-called "Wesleyan quadrilateral": scripture, tradition, experience, and reason—factors relied upon, with or without acknowledgement, in virtually all Christian theological inquiry.

FUNCTIONAL DIFFERENTIATION IN THE "QUADRILATERAL"

The 1972 statement was often criticized, and is still criticized, not just for eroding the distinction between doctrine and theology, but for failing to distinguish adequately among the particular roles to be played in theological reflection by scripture, tradition, reason, and experience. The criticism has often been couched in terms of the proper weight to be given to these factors: the fear is often expressed that two of the factors may be played off against the other two in a stalemate, or that three of the factors may gang up on the fourth. It may justly be observed that a careful reader of the 1972 statement would not arrive at such a conclusion. The statement clearly and repeatedly affirms the primacy of scripture (this is no innovation in 1988), and all four factors are described in such a way that an attentive reader could be expected to gain some sense of their distinctive roles in the process. But readers and interpreters are not always careful; and this fact, together with the relative brevity of the statement's descriptions of the four factors and the use of identical terms such as "source" and "guideline" for all four, undoubtedly led to problems. Here again, the 1988 statement represents a genuine improvement, I believe. The changes in substance are relatively modest, but through changes in organization and emphasis, fuller elaboration of the meaning of each factor, some terminological clarification, and some additional attention to the interaction of the four, the current statement is able to provide much more effective guidance.

H. Richard Niebuhr was wont to say that discussions of the authority of scripture inevitably founder when the question is framed in quantitative terms: How much authority does scripture have? Our penchant for oppositional thinking kicks in at that point, and we develop a continuum along which to range ourselves. Conservatives get described as those who think scripture has a whole lot of authority (maybe all the authority there is), while liberals are typed as those who think it doesn't have very much authority (if any at all). Niebuhr believed that the discussions become much more interesting and fruitful if the question is framed in qualitative rather than quantitative terms: What *kind* of authority does scripture have? That is, what is it authoritative for, how does that authority work, and how is it best described?[6] Our current statement on "Doctrinal Standards and Our Theological Task" portrays the authority of scripture in more than one way—a fact that I take as evidence, not of the statement's confusion or indecisiveness, but rather of the complexity of the subject, and of the variety of reasonable construals of

---

6. For Niebuhr's distinction, see the introduction by James M. Gustafson in Niebuhr's *The Responsible Self*. I have pursued these questions to some extent elsewhere, for example, in "Hermeneutics and the Authority of Scripture" and "On Being Known," in *An Invitation to Theological Study*, 55–82; and in chapter 5 of this work, "Scripture, Authenticity, and Truth."

scriptural authority that we might need to do it justice. The statement then goes on to differentiate the roles of the other three factors in theological reflection in some helpful ways. The notion that these four constitute a "quadrilateral" of roughly equivalent theological "sources" is thereby seriously called into question.

PRIMACY OF SCRIPTURE

As I just noted, the primacy of scripture was affirmed by the 1972 statement. The 1988 statement, through its fuller discussion of the distinctive functions of the four elements, permits a better understanding of what that might mean. The idea of the primacy of scripture is not well conveyed through images of ranking or weight, but rather through the sort of discussion of the *use* of scripture in theological reflection that the statement introduces and invites. The 1988 statement's section on scripture—about a page and a half in length—would in itself be a very useful text for a fuller exploration of this issue, among church leaders or in congregations.

As I read or hear expressions of opinion about the state of United Methodist doctrine and theology, I sometimes have the impression that the 1988 revision of our doctrinal and theological statement has been virtually ignored, and that people are continuing to inveigh against, or to defend, what they take to be the import of the original 1972 statement. If the newer statement is being ignored, perhaps it is because its more thorough and discriminating treatment of both doctrine and theology threatens to destabilize the pattern of binary thinking on which we seem to rely.

4

WORD of GOD and TRUTH

THE ARTICULATION OF Christian belief and witness, from New Testament times onward, has involved assertions of many different sorts. They range from straightforward historical claims, such as "Paul wrote this," to anthropological generalizations ("All have sinned" [Rom 2:23]), metaphysical and cosmological statements, and many others. Included is a variety of complex theological utterances which have at least the form of assertions, such as "God was in Christ reconciling the world to himself" (2 Cor 5:19), and "One who loves is born of God and knows God" (1 John 4:7). These diverse sorts of statements would not all seem to be of the same degree of importance or centrality to Christian witness; they manifest different kinds and levels of reflectivity, and they respond to differing needs.

The common persistence of this evident diversity throughout the Christian tradition means that there can be no *general* characterization and vindication (or demolition) of the cognitive claims involved in Christian discourse as such. The meaning and truth of any of these assertions can only be assessed in the light of the criteria relevant to its particular use. The historical claim that Paul wrote Galatians, or that Jesus was crucified, for example, is subject to the same sort of critical testing to which any other assertion of historical fact must be open. It cannot be held exempt from such examination simply because it occurs within a theological or religious context, without forfeiting its identity as a historical assertion. Of course, a theologian or a believer might want to say something which sounds like a historical assertion without meaning it as one, much as a storyteller might, but that is another matter. If an utterance is meant as a historical claim, its very meaningfulness, no less than its truth-value, depends upon its being subject in principle to the normal canons of historical inquiry. The same sort of point may be made concerning assertions of other types occurring within a theological context: each is subject to examination according to the criteria governing assertions of its type.

The difficulty of "placing" some of the assertions encountered in Christian discourse so as to determine the relevant criteria of interpretation—and indeed, the difficulty of determining whether a particular utterance actually functions as an assertion at all—is notorious. Among the most resistant to analysis in this regard are some of the complex sorts of theological utterance of which two examples were cited above: utterances which relate God in particular ways to particular events and persons. Many statements concerning the atoning work of Christ fall into this category. "In Christ God was reconciling..." (2 Cor 5:19), "Christ died for our sins" (1 Cor 15:3), and "God has brought you to life with Christ, having forgiven us all our sins" (Col 2:13) combine references to real persons and historical occasions with claims concerning

God's action or disposition. Not long ago, a recognition of the centrality of such statements to the traditional Christian witness of faith provoked considerable attention to the problematic character of claims about "acts of God": What is meant or implied by the assertion that God has acted or is present in a particular event? How is such an assertion warranted? How may one presume to claim (even if that claim takes the form of "confession") that a given historical occurrence has a particular significance in the divine economy?

The aim of this essay is to suggest a way in which the meaning and truth-value of some such utterances might be clarified by taking as an interpretative clue one of the oldest and most common ways in which Christians have characterized the language of scripture and proclamation, namely, as "Word of God." While the notion of "acts of God" directs our attention to the events purportedly described and interpreted by the language, the term "Word of God" functions to remind us of the character of the language itself. This assumes, of course, that to say, "this is the Word of God," in a theological (or liturgical) context may be to say something more than "this is true" or "this is very important." Undeniably the statement, "this is the Word of God," is often made to advance precisely those claims, that is, to lend credibility or force to what is being said or read. And certainly either or both of those claims may be implied on a particular occasion by the statement. But these familiar associations should not be allowed to obscure the possibility that the prior function of that characterization is to say something about the *sort* of utterance we have before us; that is, that whatever else might rightly be said about the nature or provenance of the statement, it is to be regarded as a word from God. That affirmation has some interesting and perhaps important features, even apart from the presumption that whatever God says is bound to be both true and important.

What sort of difference might it make to our understanding of an utterance to identify God as its speaker or author? In some cases, it might make little or no difference. There are statements whose meaning is relatively or even wholly independent of the identity of those who utter them. An assertion such as "Abraham Lincoln was born in Massachusetts" is of this sort. There are other assertions whose meaning is governed in part by the identity of the speaker: "I was born in Massachusetts," or "My brother is the President," for example. The truth-value of a statement of this second sort may not be determined until its meaning is more clearly specified, i.e., by establishing the identity of the speaker to whatever extent is necessary to make a judgment possible. (It should be clear, incidentally, that not all "self-involving" assertions require this sort of specification of authorship before their truth-value can be determined. "My sister is the President" is false if it can be proven that "the President" does not refer to anyone's sister.)

Now, surely, even if God were to make an empirical assertion of either of these sorts, that assertion would be subject to the same standards of meaning and truth which apply to anyone else's similar utterance. If God were to claim that Paul died in Rome, the claim would be true as a historical assertion only if Paul did in fact die in Rome. God's claiming it would not make it true if Paul actually died elsewhere; nor would God's claim be meaningful as a historical assertion if the fact that Paul died elsewhere were not allowed to count against the claim that he died in Rome. (Faced with the divine claim under those circumstances, we would probably be inclined to probe its meaning further, on the assumption that we have not yet understood what is really being said.) Similarly, "I led Israel out of Egypt" would be a meaningful assertion only if "Israel's leaving Egypt" were a conceivable event and if some sense might be given to the notion of the speaker's "leading" someone. (Here, the question as to how the concept, "act of God," is to be understood is pertinent.) The fact that this assertion has the first-person form of God's own claim, rather than the form of someone's claim about God, does not substantially alter the criteria by which its meaningfulness, meaning, and truth-value must be determined. It should be clear that the issue here is not God's veracity, but how our language may be understood. And the point is that to call assertions of these kinds the "Word of God" may not shed much light upon their intelligibility, or shift the ground of interpretation radically.

But there are other cases in which that designation may prove to be more interesting and more pertinent to our understanding of what is said. Consider such statements as "I love you," "I forgive you," "I consider the matter closed," and "I hope to return." None of these statements may be taken simply as a report upon an observable state of affairs; each involves some element of self-disclosure or self-commitment. Some statements of this general sort might be classified as "performative utterances," following J. L. Austin: statements which are most usefully regarded as acts rather than as assertions, and in judging which a person looks to the conditions which would make them effectual ("felicitous") rather than to the evidence which would make them true.[1] "I find you guilty,"

1. Austin, *How to Do Things with Words*.

"I promise to attend," and "Strike two!" have this performative character. "I forgive" may, in some contexts, function as a performative, indeed, even with a legally binding force, as when one forgives a debt or an obligation.

But there are also contexts in which "I forgive you" (or, perhaps more clearly, "I have forgiven you") is not so much an act as a disclosure. It may, like a performative utterance, change the situation and put things on a different footing, but it does so by telling the hearer how things stand. In this, it is closer to "I love you" than to "I commend you," and closer to "I intend to come" than to "I promise to come." It is the self-disclosive element in these utterances involving the concepts of forgiving, loving, intending, hoping, considering, identifying and so on, which needs further elucidation in connection with our inquiry.

Take the statement, "I wish it hadn't happened." It seems fair to regard this as an informative, rather than performative, utterance. Whatever its causes or effects might be, it appears to be an assertion. Its claim may be true or false. Further, it appears to be a factual assertion, one whose truth or falsity is contingent upon circumstances which could be otherwise; and a hearer may conceive of evidence which would tend to support or disconfirm the claim—e.g., the speaker's apparent mood, how the speaker proceeds to deal with the situation, or whether the speaker had tried to prevent the thing from happening. Yet, the statement is not properly viewed as a *report*, either as to outward circumstances or to the occurrence within the speaker of a phenomenon called "wishing." ("I was there when it happened" might serve as a report of the first kind; "I was frightened when it happened," of the second.) If I truthfully say "I wish it hadn't happened," I am not issuing a report, but instead I am telling my hearer something about myself. It is an informative claim about myself: stating it does not make it true, and my hearer may quite properly expect my behavior to bear out the claim in appropriate ways, or at least not to conflict with it.[2] In a similar way, "I consider you my friend" does not refer to some antecedent event or situation (that is, it is not a report on the observable facts of our relationship, nor on the inner dynamics of "considering"), nor is it best viewed as a performative statement (that is, although the utterance may surely have some effect, it does not "make" you my friend). Rather, it is a self-disclosive assertion: I am revealing, or at least claiming to reveal, something of myself to you. The revelation may lead you to rethink some incidents in our relationship up to this point, as well as perhaps to modify your attitudes toward me and your expectations of me from now on.

It is in connection with assertions of this general character that the designation of a body of discourse as "Word of God" may become most significant. To construe an utterance not only as God's word but also as God's self-disclosure is to make an important interpretative decision; it is to place the assertions contained in that discourse in such a way as to open up a certain range of criteria of interpretation and appraisal, and to render certain other criteria less pertinent.

Needless to say, that may take a bit of construing. A great amount of the material Christians characterize as "Word of God" is, prima facie, someone else's words, not only in that these texts have human authors but also in that they are often *about* God: God is spoken of in the third person, frequently

---

2. For an illuminating discussion of "telling," see Hunter, *Essays after Wittgenstein*, 91–114.

in statements having the form of empirical assertions. To take these texts as, nevertheless, God's own self-disclosive utterance, is to make what may appear to be an eccentric judgment in the face of some obvious and perhaps more immediately compelling alternatives. But there is a logic to such construal.

As a first step toward the clarification of that logic, a simple case may be useful. Suppose I say, "Ann intends to finish the job." I may have formed a hypothesis concerning Ann's intentions, which I am thus expressing; or, I may be telling you what Ann has told me. A statement as to another's intentions, attitudes, or inclinations may be a judgment based on one's knowledge of the person (or of "human nature" under the circumstances, or of whatever other data one considers relevant to such a judgment). I may be "reading" Ann's intentions from her behavior, or making an inference from past experience. But such a statement may also be simply the reiteration of what the person in question has told the speaker. I may be sharing with you what Ann said to me as to her own intentions. If so, since my statement takes the direct form it does ("Ann intends . . ."), I am probably fairly confident that her declaration to me is reliable; otherwise, I might say instead, "Ann said she intended . . . ," thus putting the burden on her. But as it stands, my statement might rightly be construed as my transmittal of Ann's own self-disclosing statement.

Now, to take "God loves you" as a word from God means to take it not as someone's hypothesis concerning God's disposition, but as a reliable transmittal or reiteration of God's own self-declaration on the matter. That is a fairly straightforward instance, parallel to "Ann intends . . ." Consider what happens when we apply this same sort of construal to other, more complex assertions, for instance, regarding the identity and work of Christ. "God was in Christ reconciling the world to himself," heard as a self-disclosive word of God, becomes revelatory of the significance *to God* of a particular historical event. It declares God's self-identification with what went on in that event: God interprets the event to us as God's own action, the fulfillment of God's own intention. The statement is no longer heard simply as someone's hypothesis about the significance of Christ, still less as a metaphysical claim about the nature (or natures) of Christ. "Christ died for our sins" becomes, not someone's inference concerning the meaning of Christ's death, but God's own disclosure of God's judgment regarding its significance—God's judgment being, in this instance, the judgment that counts. "In him all the fullness of God was pleased to dwell" (Col 1:19), taken as God's word, discloses God's self-actuation in and solidarity with this human life: Jesus is the one with whose life God is fully identified. To hear the claim that we have died with Christ as God's word is to hear God's declaration that our death is somehow included in his. In each of these cases, our attention is directed not to some unusual feature of an event, some quality inherent in the event itself that we might, in principle, find out for ourselves if we studied the event long enough or with the right equipment, but instead to what God alone can tell us about its significance. God alone can tell us this, not because God is in a better position to view the event and all its effects, but because God has freely created its significance, in the unity of God's action and self-disclosive word.

These construals are, obviously, rough and tentative and partial, and are not meant to stake out substantive Christological positions. They are intended only to suggest a direction in interpretation. Examples from areas other than Christology might serve as well. In fact, a large proportion of the typical assertions concerning "God's action in history" might be usefully approached in this way. To identify a particular event, e.g., the Exodus, as an act of God, would then not be a way of drawing attention to unusual, perhaps supernatural or miraculous features of the event, on the basis of which one might infer that God was at work in it. Instead, it would be to say that God has identified this event as an enactment of the divine intention. It is God's word that discloses the significance of the event by claiming it in a particular way. Once that identification is made—and perhaps only then—the event itself becomes disclosive of the character or purposes of God. In addition to its own value simply as the event it is, it takes on the character of a gesture or sign, because God has given it this meaning.

It is in some such ways as these, then, that the reminder that a given utterance is to be taken as "Word of God" may open some lines of interpretation. But how does that reminder bear upon the further question as to the truth of these assertions? To identify a given assertion as a self-disclosing utterance does not rob it of truth-value. It does not cease to be an assertion on that account. But a different range of truth-criteria comes into play than would be the case if we were to take the assertion as, say, an empirical hypothesis.

If my statement as to Ann's intention to "finish the job" were in fact a judgment I had formed on the basis of observing her work, it would be pertinent to the assessment of my claim to ask me to cite the evidence I considered relevant: what data do I read as reliable indicators of her intention? But, if my statement is simply a restatement of Ann's own declaration, a different set of considerations becomes involved: Is her statement of intention trustworthy (or was it a joke, a lie, a rash promise)? Can we believe her? It may also be important to know whether she is capable of fulfilling her intention, but at this point it is the intention, not its performance, which is at issue. And while we might appeal to various sorts of evidence to justify our confidence or lack of confidence in the truthfulness of her declaration, the evidence may never be wholly unambiguous. (Not even Ann's completion of her job would necessarily eliminate the possibility of doubt as to her present intention.) We may decide to believe her, or to doubt her, or to reserve judgment; what we may not do is gain some immediate access to her intention, apart from her own disclosure of it.

To take the utterances of Christian scripture or proclamation as the word of God involves a similar shift in truth-criteria. When we take a statement such as "God was in Christ" as an assertion of Paul or of another human being—certainly a reasonable thing to do—it is reasonable to expect the one making the assertion to be able to provide some evidence to support the claim: how did the writer arrive at that judgment? And certainly, that particular claim has been elucidated and defended in a great variety of ways in every period of Christian history, by thinkers who acknowledged the validity of that expectation. Even Paul would not spurn such a request—though the inquirer is likely to find that Paul chiefly advances and defends his claims concerning Christ, not on the basis of empirical evidence, nor through metaphysical argument, but on the basis of what he has heard God say through the prophets and through the church's tradition ("from the Lord"). But to take the claim as the word of God introduces a new element: in addition to (or perhaps despite) whatever the relevant evidence may indicate, we have God's word for it; or at least, that is what the designation, "Word of God," asserts. We face the claim directly, not as a hypothesis put forward by a third party, but as a putative self-revelatory assertion.

In such a case, it is to the consequences of the claim, rather than to its antecedent grounds, that we must look for confirmation of its truthfulness, and sometimes for a clearer indication of its meaning as well. The truth of the statements "I love you" or "I have forgiven you" will be borne out, or not, by the course of the relationship between speaker and hearer from that point on. The claim generates a certain range of expectations. If the expectations, by and large, seem to be fulfilled by the later course of developments, the hearer is generally satisfied (and properly justified) to take this as confirmation of the claim. If certain expectations, especially the more crucial ones in the hearer's judgment, are unfulfilled or thwarted, the hearer may conclude either that the claim was untrue, or that its meaning was misunderstood. Either conclusion may lead to some sort of confrontation in which the situation is clarified. ("How can you say you love me, when . . . ?" "Is this what you call 'forgiving someone'?!") It is not at all uncommon for our expectations in connection with such claims to be modified considerably over the course of a relationship—some receding, others assuming new importance, fresh ones appearing. One major reason for this is that it is in such relationships that we learn, and continue to learn, the meaning of concepts like "love" and "forgiveness." The process of understanding and the process of confirmation are inseparable.

This is clearly the case with the assertions we have been considering as divine self-disclosure. Their meaning and truth may only be assessed through a continual process of discovering and testing their implications. This involves, in part, becoming educated in the meaning of, e.g., divine love or forgiveness, or divine judgment or presence, so as to learn what sorts of expectations are justified and what sorts are inappropriate in this context. What does it mean, for example, to have God present? Can the divine presence be sensed? How does it differ from divine absence? When is it useful to speak of God's presence? Of course, one can hardly learn the right use of such a term apart from the matrix of discourse in which it is imbedded: a working knowledge of the notion of God's presence involves a familiarity with certain features of Christian affirmation regarding creation, providence, the human condition, and so on. Furthermore, a person does not gain mastery of any of these concepts one at a time, moving on, say, from divine grace to divine judgment and then to divine righteousness. Rather, one gradually learns a whole way of thinking, speaking, and existing, in which these terms and concepts figure significantly, interpreting one another and together giving a certain sense to life.

This leads to another feature of this process of discovery and examination: Besides requiring an immersion in a whole field of discourse, rather than the dissection of isolated concepts, it also involves a willingness to have one's expectations in connection with divine love or presence or judgment put to the test by directing one's life accordingly. This is because it is in the course of that sort of living interaction that we may come to learn (to put it very simply) what *God* means by "love" and "forgiveness" and "faithfulness." If the assertions in question are to be taken as divine self-disclosure, rather than only as human opinions about God, it would seem that the most obvious context in which to pursue the question of their meaning and validity would be the ongoing divine-human relationship itself. It is as that relationship is lived out that we gain and refine our understanding of God's own word. Again, the procedure through which we come to understand the meaning of that word and the procedure of confirmation may fairly be said to coincide. We cannot judge the truth of a self-revelatory claim until we know its meaning, and we cannot learn its meaning until we are engaged in the same living practice of conceptual discovery and formation which also leads to judgments of confirmation or disconfirmation.

To hear an utterance as the word of God is, at least in the sorts of cases considered here, to hear it as an "address," in which God becomes present to the hearer and offers thereby the possibility of new understanding and appropriate response. It conveys a claim to truth; that is an inescapable feature of its meaning. But it does not simply seek to inform; it also invites the hearer into a relationship which, among other things, is to be the context for a continuing exploration of the meaning and truth of that divine self-disclosure. Such is the invitation which calls the Christian community into being. Christian theology is one aspect of that community's ongoing response.

5

SCRIPTURE, AUTHENTICITY, and TRUTH

"DOES THE CLAIM that the Bible has authority any longer make sense?"[1] Robin Scroggs, posing this question in a recent article, answers it in the negative. According to Scroggs, most church people have what he calls a "legal" understanding of authority: To say that the Bible is authoritative is to say "that the statements of the texts, both ethical and theological, are binding on believers of all times. A Christian is obliged to believe what the Bible says is essential to faith and to perform what the Bible says one must do or not do."[2] Observing that most Christians, whether conservative or liberal, do not in fact treat the Bible as authoritative in this way, he contends that the term "authority" ought to be abandoned in discussions of the use of scripture. "My judgment," he says, "is that the recent attempts to save some meaning for the 'authority' of the Bible are no more than way-stations. I propose instead that we forthwith give up any claim that the

1. Scroggs, "Bible as Foundational Document," 19.
2. Ibid., 28.

Bible is authoritative (as I have defined the word) in guidance for contemporary faith and morals."[3]

The constructive counterpart to this proposal is that we regard the Bible as a "foundational document." What this means, for Scroggs, is that we recognize the power of the biblical texts—and, more specifically, the texts of the New Testament—to create Christian faith and to form Christian selfhood; that we give them an indispensable role as an "agenda setter for Christianity," offering both questions and answers with which Christians must somehow deal; and, further, that we acknowledge those texts as "definitional for Christianity," which means that "any contemporary statement, if it differs significantly from the New Testament 'definition,' should not call itself Christianity."[4]

There is a striking similarity between the roles assigned to the Bible in Scroggs's proposal—essentially, a "creative" role and a "definitional" role[5]—and the roles assigned to scripture in the standard discussions of biblical authority in Protestant Orthodoxy. The Lutheran and Reformed theologians of the post-Reformation era typically ascribed two kinds of authority to scripture. With respect to the first, scripture is the source of understanding (*principium cognoscendi*) in matters of faith and morals; with respect to the second, it is the canon or norm by which faith and conduct are judged in the church. The first, called "causative authority" by such Lutherans as

3. Ibid., 23.

4. Ibid., 24–25.

5. The "agenda-setting" role, as Scroggs describes it, can be assimilated to the "definitional" role: Christians, he says, are "not free to ignore" the New Testament's questions and answers, nor the centrality it gives to Jesus Christ. The implication is that if one does ignore such things, one is departing from Christianity.

Scripture, Authenticity, and Truth   59

David Hollaz, and known by other names (sometimes simply as "divine authority") among the Reformed theologians, was (to follow Hollaz) that "by which scripture generates and confirms in the human mind assent to the things to be believed."[6] It is the "illuminating power" that begets faith by bringing the reader or hearer to understanding; it is scripture's capacity to teach, to convey the knowledge of God. These writers generally related this first kind of scriptural authority closely to the *testimonium internum Spiritus Sancti*.[7] Further criteria, both internal and external, were often adduced in support of this authority, but these were normally regarded as "auxiliary proofs of lesser value."[8] It is scripture's own power to bring us to the knowledge of God, to awaken faith and transform our existence, which constitutes its causative authority.

The second kind of authority, called "normative authority" or "canonical authority" by these writers, is displayed in the use of the Bible in the church as the norm or judge of doctrine. The church appeals to scripture, as the rule of faith and morals, to resolve controversies, or to measure the adequacy of a statement. (Much attention was given by these Protestants to defending the principle that it is scripture, and not some other authority, that is the supreme judge in such matters. Although it is true in one sense that the church judges *by* scripture, still it is scripture that is the judge. Its interpreters are subject to

6. ". . . qua scriptura assensum credendorum in intellectu hominis generat et confirmat." Quoted in Schmid, *Die Dogmatik der evangelisch-lutherischen Kirche*, 48 (ET: 104). I have not followed the Hay-Jacobs translation here.

7. Schmid, *Dogmatik*, 55 (ET: 63); Heppe, *Die Dogmatik der evangelisch-reformierten Kirche*, 21 (ET: 23).

8. Heppe, *Dogmatik*, 21 (ET: 23). Cf. Pöhlmann, *Abriss der Dogmatik*, 46–47.

its authority.[9]) For the Protestant Orthodox writers, the normative or canonical authority of scripture is grounded in the same "internal" character and power which is constitutive of its causative authority. God (and not, say, the decision of a church body to regard it as such) is the source of scripture's normative as well as of its causative authority.[10] The church does not bestow this authority, but only acknowledges it.

The idea of scripture's causative authority seems quite consonant with Scroggs's first recommendation, namely, that rather than think of biblical authority in some "legal" sense, commanding us to believe, we simply allow the texts to do their work, and thus to elicit our belief. "To release the texts from an external, authoritative power," says Scroggs, "releases the power internal to the texts to come to life and to function to change *by persuasion* our being, our thinking, and our action."[11] Indeed, the "legal" sense of biblical authority that Scroggs rejects looks as much out of keeping with the formal concept of causative authority in these writers as it is with our modern commitments. The idea of normative or canonical authority, on the other hand, seems to echo in Scroggs's notion of the "definitional" role of scripture (or, rather, of the New Testament). Here, one might say, ideas of what is genuinely Christian are "ruled in" or "ruled out"; scripture is functioning in a regulative way.

---

9. See, for example, Turretin, *Institutes of Elenctic Theology*, 154–62.

10. Richard A. Muller quotes the English writer Edward Leigh as representative on this point: "From the divine flows the canonical authority of the Scripture." Muller, *Post-Reformation Reformed Dogmatics*, 2:378.

11. Scroggs, 24.

Scripture, Authenticity, and Truth   61

At this point, however, one encounters another striking feature of Scroggs's proposal, something that differentiates it crucially from the Protestant Orthodox treatments. Whereas the latter offer explicit theological rationales for the roles scripture is to play in the church, Scroggs omits any such rationale. He deliberately avoids grounding these uses of scripture theologically, apparently in the hope of avoiding what he calls "theological imperialism."[12] It is characteristic that Scroggs's only reference to the idea of the internal testimony of the Holy Spirit is a warning against the misuse of claims to have the Spirit's authority for one's interpretation.[13] He keeps the discussion entirely on a functional level.

The contrast is even more pronounced when we turn from the "creative" to the "definitional" power of scripture. For Scroggs, the New Testament is definitive of Christianity because it is the "foundational document" of the Christian movement. "What any movement 'means' is always set by the parameters of its foundational documents."[14] But there is an ambiguity to the term "foundational document(s)." If a movement's "foundational documents" are simply the writings associated with the movement's beginnings, then Scroggs's statement appears to be an unwarranted generalization. Nothing prevents later writings from superseding earlier ones and coming to be definitive of a movement. A certain amount of this seems to have happened in the case of the formation of the New Testament itself: some early writings were preserved more or less intact, others were discarded after being used in various ways as sources in the composition

12. Ibid., 23.
13. Ibid., 22.
14. Ibid., 25.

of new texts, others were simply lost, and so forth. The earlier writings of a movement do not necessarily have a continuing "definitional" power. Where they do not, we might regard those earlier writings as "founding documents" in some way, but they would not be "foundational documents" in the sense in which Scroggs uses that term. For Scroggs, "foundational documents" appears to mean not just "founding documents," but early writings which continue to exercise a normative role for the movement. In other words, he means "authoritative writings"—even though the character and ground of that authority are left unspecified.

Scroggs observes that there are other uses of the term "authority" than the one he is rejecting, and that, given a broader sense of the term, his proposal might be construed as a proposal concerning the authority of scripture. It is the rigidity of the prevailing understanding which leads him to avoid the term.[15] But in dismissing the term, and the narrow "legal" understanding he thinks inextricably tied to it, he may also be giving up some important resources for critical reflection on the character and function of scripture, and for combating authoritarian misuses of scripture.[16] It might be better to acknowledge, with David H. Kelsey, that "'authoritative' is part of the meaning of 'scripture.'"[17] Rather than abandoning the term "authority" to authoritarian uses, a more promising course might be a fuller exploration of the concept with

15. Ibid., 28.

16. In an influential essay, Carl J. Friedrich identifies the "potentiality of reasoned elaboration" as intrinsic to the concept of authority, and as something that distinguishes genuine authority from its counterfeits (for instance, from authoritarian conduct). Friedrich, "Authority, Reason, and Discretion," 35ff.

17. Kelsey, *Uses of Scripture in Recent Theology*, 97.

which the term is rightly associated, in the interest of a more adequate general account of the authority of scripture. This essay is intended as a step in that direction.

I.

Some very useful resources for such an exploration have been provided by recent philosophical treatments of the concept, and in particular by the work of Richard T. De George. In *The Nature and Limits of Authority*, De George aims to present an understanding of authority which does not take political or legal authority as the paradigm case, as many influential earlier treatments do. His treatment is remarkable in its scope and subtlety, in its sensitivity to shades of difference among uses, and in its patience with ambiguity.

Rather than begin with a definition of authority or with a particular instance serving as a paradigm, De George begins with an abstract formulation of what he calls "the authority relation": "someone or something (X) is an authority if he (she, or it) stands in relation to someone else (Y) as superior stands to inferior with respect to some realm, field, or domain (R)."[18] He takes this as a "working model" which "handles the more obvious cases," and which can be amplified and corrected as required. Notably absent from it are some of the terms commonly employed in definitions of authority, such as "right," "power," "command," and "obey." What we have instead is a relation of inequality between two parties with respect to some "realm, field, or domain." Whether and how that relationship in a particular instance involves rights,

18. De George, *Nature and Limits of Authority*, 14.

powers, obligations, actions of one party upon another, and so forth depends on features yet to be specified.

Several features of this formulation should be noted. First, as the pronouns in parentheses imply, things as well as persons may be authorities (or bearers of authority), but those subject to authority are always persons.[19] Second, the authority relation always involves inequality. The inequality is not normally absolute. Its scope is limited to the relevant domain. It is not necessarily permanent. But it is real. (Another contemporary philosopher, E. D. Watt, has brought out this feature memorably: "Authority is never egalitarian. An authority is always a superior of some kind, to be obeyed in some cases, in other cases to be followed, consulted, attended to, deferred to, or conformed to. . . . Authority in all its forms is associated with, and is a constant reminder of, some human limitation, weakness, or dependence."[20]) Third, as already noted, the authority relation obtains within some specifiable "realm, field, or domain." X may be in authority over Y in certain respects, say, as the latter's commanding military officer; at the same time, Y may be an authority for X in certain respects, say, in the field of engine repair. To say "X is an authority," without further elaboration, is not very illuminating, unless the context supplies the missing information: An authority in relation to whom? In what domain? Answers to these questions will begin to flesh out the specific kind of authority being claimed.

19. "An authority might be not only a person, but also possibly a thing, such as a book or the law, and in such instances it is not inappropriate to say that the person stands in an inferior relation to the thing. . . . Those subject to authority, on the other hand, are not things" ibid., 16.

20. Watt, *Authority*, 7.

Scripture, Authenticity, and Truth 65

Ordinarily, those answers will indicate implicitly which of the two major types of authority the authority in question belongs to. De George calls these two types "executive" and "nonexecutive" authority. "In general, an executive authority has the right or power to act for or on someone else. A nonexecutive authority does not."[21] The two types may be combined in the same bearer of authority, and this may lead to some confusion at times as to the properties of each. De George notes that the basic distinction he proposes is in some ways similar to that drawn by R. S. Peters between someone's being "in authority" and someone's being "an authority"; those locutions point to one way the distinction is acknowledged in everyday usage.[22]

Nonexecutive authority, as a type, includes at least the following kinds: the authority of knowledge, or epistemic authority; the authority of competence; the authority of example, or exemplary authority; and the authority of authenticity or excellence. Some of these kinds may be instances of others. For example, all the others mentioned might be treated as subdivisions of the authority of competence; or epistemic authority might be taken as the broader category, inclusive of the others. Any such arrangement of these varieties depends upon one's concepts of knowledge, competence, and so forth.

Executive authority, on the other hand, is "the right or power of someone (X) to do something (S) in some realm, field, or domain (R), in a context (C)."[23] It too may be distinguished into kinds ("imperative," or the authority to command,

21. De George, *Nature and Limits of Authority*, 22.
22. Peters, "Symposium: Authority," 207–24, esp. 209–15.
23. De George, *Nature and Limits of Authority*, 17.

and "performatory," or the authority "to perform some action other than commanding"[24]) and further specified according to the realm or context involved (familial, political, religious, and so forth). De George notes that the bearer of executive authority need not be a personal agent. Even though speaking of an impersonal object—for example, a text or a body of rules—as "commanding" or "doing" something involves a stretching of our language, we frequently do speak thus. In so doing, we may be unconsciously bearing witness to the inevitable social context and character of all authority.[25]

The discussion of authority requires some further terms and conceptual distinctions beyond these divisions into types and classes and the specification of realms and contexts. De George takes up the common distinction between *de facto* and *de jure* authority in connection with another pair of terms, legitimate and illegitimate authority. X is a *de facto* authority (or has *de facto* authority) for Y in R if Y behaves toward X accordingly. X is a *de jure* authority (or has *de jure* authority) if X's authority is held and exercised in accord with a set of principles or laws obtaining in the social context. To observe that X has *de jure* authority, however, is not to claim that X's authority is legitimate. It may be "legitimated," in a descriptive sociological sense, by being *de jure*, but De George reserves the term "legitimate" for authority that is "grounded" or justified: "legitimate" is, then, a prescriptive term. The criteria for legitimate authority will vary considerably with the kind and situation. To say that X's authority is only *de facto* and not *de jure* is not to say that it is illegitimate. Authority may be either *de facto* or *de jure*, or both, or neither. It may be either

24. Ibid., 63.
25. Ibid., 64.

Scripture, Authenticity, and Truth 67

legitimate or illegitimate. Further, authority may be held legitimately, but exercised in an illegitimate fashion.[26]

The consideration of an example will help to give substance to these points, and will also prepare the way for an application to the question of the authority of the Bible. J.B. is a high school biology teacher. She is a *de facto* epistemic authority for her students in biology to the extent that they are willing to believe what she tells them about the subject. In their willingness to believe her, the students are not necessarily gullible or credulous. They may (let us imagine) have satisfied themselves as to her credentials, and checked with experts in the field who were able to testify to her reliability. It is more likely that they are relying—with some justification—on the procedures by which J.B. was appointed to her teaching post, or on their previous experiences with teachers. They may exercise some discrimination in their willingness to believe, reserving judgment on some points while accepting others, and so on. In any case, they are relying upon her superior knowledge of the field. She cannot function as an epistemic authority for them if they think they know as much about the subject as she does. (They are also relying upon her veracity; she cannot function as an epistemic authority for them if they believe she is lying to them, withholding important data, misleading them, and so on. In such a case, even though they might grant that she has superior knowledge of the field, they would not accept her authority. She would not

---

26. Ibid., 18–20. De George introduces some further terms and distinctions, such as that between effective and ineffective authority and between the extent and the intensity of authority, but these need not concern us here.

be a *de facto* epistemic authority for them. The "authority relation," to use De George's term, would be corrupted or lost.)

In addition to her authority of knowledge, J.B. possesses *de facto* authority of competence for her students in biology if they tend to behave as she recommends in order to accomplish some purpose relevant to their mastery of the subject. Teaching is not merely the imparting of information, and learning is not merely the accepting of information. J.B.'s work as a teacher may include teaching her students procedures of investigation through laboratory observation or experimentation. She may ask them to follow certain steps in working with a specimen, perhaps repeating the process on several occasions. In doing so, her aim is not simply to have them follow the steps, but to help them acquire a certain discipline of observation, and perhaps to "catch on" to some aspect of what the science of biology involves.

J.B. holds *de facto* exemplary authority for her students as well if, rather than just telling them what they should do, she demonstrates by doing it, and they imitate her actions. This might pertain to a laboratory session or some other fairly restricted context, or it might be more general in scope, so that the students learn the subject in large part by following along. (To what extent this is an important pedagogical element, and what it involves, varies with the subjects, teachers, students, and contexts involved.) She may even come to hold what De George calls the authority of authenticity if her students take her to represent a kind of excellence to which they might aspire—as a scientist, as a teacher, or as a human being—and set about not just to become "like her" in some self-constricting fashion but to achieve in themselves the excellence she represents.

All these are kinds of nonexecutive authority, held *de facto*. At least some of these kinds may also be held *de jure*, and in this example some are. J.B.'s authority of knowledge and competence are *de jure*, in De George's terms, in that she presumably holds an academic degree and other forms of certification, and has been duly appointed to her teaching post. In these ways her epistemic authority in the field and her authority of competence as a teacher in the field have been publicly acknowledged *de jure*.[27] One might say that her exemplary authority is also a *de jure* authority, to the extent that it can be subsumed under the authority of competence or combined with it in some fuller understanding of the nonexecutive authority involved in the teacher-student relationship. The authority of authenticity, as De George describes it, would be less susceptible to regularization, at least in this context.

When the authority of knowledge and of competence are thus given *de jure* recognition, this does not turn them into forms of executive authority. As an epistemic authority, even if that authority is recognized *de jure*, J.B. does not have

27. It may seem that the concept of *de jure* authority implies authorization, so that, for example, *de jure* epistemic authority is "authorized authority." But it is not clear that the idea of authorization is helpful in this context. Normally, one is authorized to do something. Nonexecutive authority is not an authority to do anything. The certification of epistemic authority would not, in itself, authorize the bearer to do anything. Such certification might be a prerequisite for the bestowal of executive authority, but in itself it is not so much an act of authorization as one of recognition. On the other hand, if an act of certification does involve authorization to do something, it has become more than the certification of nonexecutive authority; it has become the conferral of executive authority, however weak or ambiguous. (The executive authority conferred by an academic degree is a case in point.) The idea of *de jure* epistemic authority requires some careful "fencing" if it is not to be misunderstood.

the right or power to require her students to believe what she says, or even to listen to her. Her authority of competence does not entitle her to order her students to follow certain procedures. The nonexecutive authority of a teacher should not be confused with the authority to teach.[28]

No doubt, J.B. does have the authority to teach, and to do a number of things pertinent to that activity. She has the authority, presumably, to design her courses (within whatever limitations are established), to arrange class activities, to give instructions, to make assignments, to set examinations, to evaluate the students' performance, and so forth. These are instances of executive authority—some "imperative" and some "performatory." In this example, this authority is held both *de facto* (insofar as students and others respond to it) and *de jure* (in that J.B. is invested with the authority by her appointment to the faculty, and the authority is articulated in the relevant laws and policies).

J.B.'s work as teacher therefore involves a complex blend of executive and nonexecutive authority of various kinds. In many of her actions in the course of the day, she may exercise two or more at once. "Do the problems on pages 97–102" is, on the face of it, an instance of executive, "imperative" authority. If a student asks "Why?" the reply might be, "Because if you don't, you'll get a zero on the assignment." But it also may involve the authority of competence, as is shown by the fact that the answer to the student's "Why?" might also be, "Because these problems are illustrative of the point we've been discussing, and working through them will help you see the difference between the two approaches we considered."

---

28. De George, *Nature and Limits of Authority*, 58–61; for the limitations on nonexecutive authority more generally, see 46–61.

Let us assume that the overall purpose of the school—the purpose to which J.B., in her teaching, wishes to contribute—is the fostering of knowledge and competence. That purpose cannot be achieved by the exercise of executive authority alone. Executive authority, whether the teacher's or others,' may insure that most of the students are physically present most of the time, that reasonable order is kept, that students do at least some of their homework, and so forth. It may, in these and other ways, help to establish the conditions under which teaching and learning can take place. (The degree to which executive authority is necessary to establish these conditions will depend on a great variety of factors.) But executive authority cannot compel learning. One cannot be compelled by executive authority to understand, any more than one can be thus compelled to believe. Executive authority may keep one at the task; it may sometimes compel behavior which leads, sooner or later, to learning and understanding. Its role in the educational process is in many cases both positive and negative. It both contributes to and detracts from the realization of the overall purpose.

J.B.'s authority of knowledge and competence are, to use De George's language, "substitutional" in nature: they "substitute the knowledge [or ability] of one person in a certain field for the lack of knowledge [or ability] of another."[29] They are also "expendable" in principle. Some of her students may go on to acquire more knowledge and competence in the field of biology than she possesses. If so, she will cease to be an authority for them. It is conceivable that they might

29. Ibid., 36–37. He makes this point explicitly concerning epistemic authority, but I believe it can be extended to the authority of competence in at least some cases.

become authorities for her. The situation with her executive authority is different in several respects. For example, it will not automatically cease as her students grow in wisdom. It will cease for them (at least *de jure*) as they leave her class or finish school, or when she resigns her position. Others might replace J.B. and exercise the executive authority she presently exercises, but it is not "substitutional" or "expendable," as De George uses these terms.

II.

How might this discussion illuminate the concept of the authority of scripture? First, and most obviously, it suggests that we would be well advised not to expect the authority of scripture to be of one kind only. Some treatments of the authority of scripture proceed as if the meaning of "authority" were clear and univocal, and the only questions with regard to scripture were whether it has any authority, and if so, how much. Other treatments, recognizing that there are different kinds of authority, proceed as if the task were to establish what kind of authority scripture has—and often, the procedure is disjunctive: "Not that kind, but this kind"—for example, "Not restrictive, but empowering." It might advance the discussion if we were to expect scripture's authority to be complex, and to ask, not "What kind?" but "What kinds? In what contexts? For what purposes?"[30]

---

30. James M. Gustafson's comments on H. Richard Niebuhr's approach to the question of the authority of scripture for Christian ethics remain valuable in this connection. See his introduction to Niebuhr's *Responsible Self*. A more recent helpful introductory analysis is Placher, "Nature of Biblical Authority."

Secondly, if we take the evident continuing viability of the Protestant Orthodox distinction between causative authority and normative authority as indicative of a basic twofold distinction among kinds of scriptural authority, it might be worthwhile to pursue the degree of correspondence between these two and De George's two basic types, nonexecutive and executive authority, respectively.[31]

The notion of causative authority would appear to fit readily within the category of nonexecutive authority, and to have close relations within that category to (at least) the concepts of epistemic authority and the authority of competence, as De George describes these. "Causative authority" may be an umbrella term for a modest variety of "authority relations" between scripture and its readers or hearers—relations in which scripture functions to bring its readers or hearers to the knowledge of God.[32] Let us take a closer look at this.

Following De George's formulation, scripture has *de facto* epistemic authority for a reader if the reader is inclined to believe what scripture says. This formulation has a misleading simplicity. Two points of clarification are in order here. First, how the reader determines "what scripture says" will

31. In what follows, I will pursue some features of possible conceptual correspondence, without delving into detailed historical analysis of the Protestant Orthodox discussion. It seems clear that the concept of causative authority was seriously compromised in its material elaboration, as well as by other components of the doctrine of scripture, as the latter developed in the post-Reformation era.

32. This is, of course, only one of several ways of describing the aim, but it is one suited to this discussion. "Knowledge" in this context need not be taken in a narrowly cognitive or rational sense, that is, in a sense that would exclude the emotions, the affections, and so on. Here as elsewhere, what "knowledge" means is in part governed by its object. As with the meaning, so with the means of attaining it.

depend upon what the reader thinks scripture is, and how the reader thinks scripture "says" anything. To accept scripture's epistemic authority is not to oblige oneself to take as true any declarative sentence one happens to find in it. That acceptance is consistent with a very broad range of possible understandings of the character of scripture, and with a very broad range of interpretative approaches.[33] One might, for example, adopt a view of scripture's proper use in which a good part of what we have to learn from scripture is not explicitly conveyed by it in some didactic fashion, but instead is generated in the reader's mind as the reader imaginatively enters the world of a scriptural narrative, or struggles with a moral problem posed by the text, or tries to reconcile conflicting scriptural portrayals of God or of the human condition. In other words, much of the teaching is indirect. In such a case, accepting the epistemic authority of scripture might amount more to a presumption that scripture has something to teach us, or that it can bring us to a knowledge that we presently lack, than to a willingness to believe what any particular text says. (The distinction between epistemic authority and the authority of competence is not altogether clear in a situation such as this, as we shall see.)

Second, as observed in the example of the biology teacher's students, "believing" can mean a variety of things, from firm conviction to provisional acceptance, and even to a tentative willingness to entertain the truth of a claim. What "believing" means depends further upon the nature of the claim, the context in which it is made, and so on. Epistemic

---

33. See Wood, "Hermeneutics and the Authority of Scripture," in *An Invitation to Theological Study*, 55–70.

authority, even as De George describes it, is thus a fairly broad concept.[34]

Part of scripture's causative authority—indeed, the major part—may be the authority of competence. Here the focus is not upon the reader's accepting what scripture teaches, but upon the reader's following scripture's recommendations in order to achieve some end. If the end is the knowledge of God, scripture exercises the authority of competence if the reader follows its precepts, adopts its advice as to how God is to be known. Here again, how the reader thinks "scripture" "recommends" or "advises" (or "admonishes" or "warns" or "encourages") depends upon a number of theological and hermeneutical decisions. The point is that scripture exercises causative authority not only when the reader is willing in some sense to believe what it says, but also when the reader is willing to undertake a heuristic course of action in accord with its recommendations.[35] Scripture may thus function indirectly to capacitate the reader, providing new competence for understanding and action, by leading the reader into forms of behavior that yield new insight.

It would be possible to speak of an exemplary authority of scripture in this connection as well, and perhaps to refine

34. See Wood, "The Knowledge Born of Obedience," in ibid., 35–44.

35. "Recommendation" and the like, rather than "directive" and the like, are in order here because the latter are usually associated with executive (imperative) authority, while the former are in keeping with the character of nonexecutive authority. Of course, the verb or grammatical mood employed does not necessarily determine or indicate the kind of authority involved. De George uses a doctor-patient relationship as an example of the authority of competence: "Despite its imperative form, the doctor's prescription is not a command but is a hypothetical statement, telling the patient what he recommends that the patient do if the patient wants to get well." De George, *Nature and Limits of Authority*, 43.

the categories beyond the treatment De George has provided. It may well be that the entire discussion should be ordered around the authority of competence, if the potential inherent in the notion of causative authority is to be realized. In any case, the main tenor of the concept of causative authority as it has been construed here is well represented in H. Richard Niebuhr's idea of what he called the "educational authority" of scripture:

> It is like the role of the teacher, which is to lead to a direct relationship of the student to the more ultimate authority of reality that the teacher mediates. It is important not because it gives us knowledge of itself, but because it gives us knowledge of God acting on men, and of ourselves before God . . . . The community cannot think the mind of Christ without the training of Scripture. . . . But Scripture always points to the authority which it mediates, and like the able teacher, seeks to make itself unnecessary.[36]

If causative authority belongs to the category of nonexecutive authority and may be associated particularly with the authority of knowledge and competence, or with what we might think of as the nonexecutive authority of a teacher, so normative or canonical authority may best be understood within the category of executive authority. Executive authority, to recall De George's formulation, is "the right or power of someone (X) to do something (S) in some realm, field, or domain (R), in a context (C)." According to the Protestant Orthodox accounts of scripture's normative authority, it is the

---

36. Gustafson, describing Niebuhr's view, in his introduction to Niebuhr's *The Responsible Self*, 23–24.

right or power of scripture to judge Christian teaching and practice. In this role, scripture is not advising, recommending, or teaching; it is judging. Advising, recommending, teaching, and the like, as they have been discussed above in the context of nonexecutive authority, are activities compatible with the concept of nonexecutive authority, where the element of authority is understood not as the authority of scripture to teach (for example), but rather as an authority that is present in the teaching relationship. The reader responds to that authority by consulting scripture, following its precepts as guides to understanding, and so on. Recall from our example that the authority of knowledge and competence is not an authority to teach. It is, rather, an authority involved in teaching and learning, present in the relationship between teacher and learner. If there is authority to teach, it is executive authority. The authority to judge, likewise, belongs to that type.

According to a broad consensus of Protestant Orthodox writers, the normative authority of scripture is (using De George's scheme) exercised in the realm of doctrine, and in the context of the church. (The realm might be specified in other ways, for example, as "faith and morals," credenda and agenda; but let us take "doctrine" as an adequate general term for our purposes.) What is to be determined by that judgment? The answer implied by the affirmation that scripture is "the only norm of doctrine in the church" and the only judge of all controversy"[37] is: whatever is relevant. It is by scripture that one determines whatever an executive judgment can determine about doctrine.

The question then becomes: What can the normative authority of scripture, construed as a kind of executive authority,

37. Preus, *Theology of Post-Reformation Lutheranism*, 303.

determine about doctrine? Simply put, it can determine doctrine itself; it can establish doctrine for the church, in the sense of establishing what the doctrine is to be. By so doing, it also determines whether any candidate for the status of doctrine actually qualifies. It distinguishes genuine doctrine from "false doctrine."

Does this mean that normative authority determines the truth of doctrine? There are some cases (some instances of "performative utterance," as J. L. Austin called them[38]) in which executive authority can make something true. If the umpire says "You're out!" you're out. Many treatments of the notion of the "word of God" in connection with scripture stress this performative aspect, showing how the gospel might be construed as a promise, for instance, or as a word of address that lays a claim on the hearer, or as a message conveying forgiveness and reconciliation. This aspect of the content and force of scripture has important implications for an understanding both of its authority and of its truth, and should be explored in any fuller construal of scripture that makes serious use of such ideas. It is unlikely, however, that the whole of Christian doctrine can rightly be construed as performative utterance, at least in any way that would eliminate the need for recourse to something other than executive authority to establish its truth.

On the whole, rather than saying that normative authority determines the truth of doctrine, it would be more accurate to say that it determines what the church shall hold to be true. It determines whether a given teaching is to be considered a teaching of the church. A term sometimes employed in this connection—for instance, in the extensive

38. Austin, *How to Do Things with Words*, 1–11.

Scripture, Authenticity, and Truth 79

treatment by William A. Christian, Sr., of the logic of these issues—is "authenticity." The question of doctrinal authenticity has the form, "Is statement *s* a doctrine of religious community *R*?"[39] A doctrine of the normative authority of scripture is, in Christian's terms, a "governing doctrine" of the Christian community concerning how that determination is to be made.

How scripture is to be brought into play to judge the authenticity of doctrine requires careful reflection. It will not do simply to suppose that if a doctrine is found in scripture, in the sense of being stated explicitly somewhere in the text, it is ipso facto authentic. Among the doctrines whose authenticity scripture is to judge are the doctrines found within scripture itself; and it is altogether possible that some of these may be judged non-authentic. To say that scripture has normative authority does not imply that every individual unit of scripture—every assertion of fact, every moral judgment, commandment, etiological tale, psalm, or what have you—has normative authority. Particular elements of scripture may have a role to play in generating theological understanding without themselves being representative of that understanding. Of course, people may grant authority to verses of scripture simply because they are part of scripture, just as people may grant authority to what celebrities say in product endorsements simply because they are celebrities. One function of a properly articulated understanding of scriptural authority is to correct such mistakes.

Although it would be more accurate to say that normative or canonical authority determines what the church shall hold to be true (that is, what shall count as authentic doctrine)

39. Christian, *Doctrines of Religious Communities*, 12–34.

than to say that it determines the truth of what is held, this formulation needs some further development. If we assume that, from the standpoint of the Christian community, a necessary condition of a doctrine's authenticity is its truth; and if the truth of a statement (with the sorts of exceptions noted above) cannot be established by executive authority; then we must also conclude that normative authority as such, while necessary to establish the authenticity of a doctrine, is not ordinarily sufficient to do so. If a doctrine advances a claim to truth, normative authority can establish the authenticity of the doctrine only on the condition that the doctrine is true. This means that a judgment of authenticity on the basis of normative authority should always be understood to have a hypothetical quality to it. Just as an official's authority to perform a marriage does not entitle her or him to marry people at random but only when certain antecedent conditions have been satisfied, so the normative authority of scripture to pronounce doctrines authentic depends upon certain conditions having been met.

This does not mean that the authority of scripture is necessarily insufficient to determine both the truth and the authenticity of doctrine, but only that the normative authority of scripture, construed strictly as executive authority, is insufficient—or would be, if it were employed in isolation from its causative authority. The nonexecutive authority of scripture, its authority of knowledge and competence—its causative authority—may be said to play a decisive role in determining the truth of doctrinal statements, and thus contributing to a determination regarding their authenticity. This seems entirely consistent with the principle encountered in the Protestant Orthodox writers that the normative authority of scripture presupposes and involves its causative authority. Whether those writers should be followed in their affirmation that scripture is the sole authority for determining either the truth or the authenticity of Christian doctrines is, of course, another question.

At the same time that causative authority is thus involved in or with normative authority, there is a way in which the normative authority of scripture may support its causative authority. Just as the executive authority operating in a school, structuring the teaching and learning relationship, can help to establish the conditions for learning, so the executive authority of scripture may help to establish the conditions under which scripture becomes an instrument of learning. H. Richard Niebuhr's idea of the "corroborative authority" of scripture—the complement to its educational authority—suggests how this might be: "It [sc. scripture] is a court of validation for the judgments and actions of the Christian community and its members. . . . The Christian community is as capable of false rationalizations, of perverted and distorted purposes, as any other community. The Bible, as the court of validation, aids the Church in eliminating its perversities, and verifying its true purposes."[40] It is the normative authority of scripture—the fact that it is definitive of the community's identity and purpose—which, so to speak, sends the members of the Christian community back to check their own perceptions of the truth against what is mediated afresh through scripture.

---

40. Gustafson, introduction to Niebuhr's *The Responsible Self*, 24.

III.

Left untouched in this exploration, except by remote implication, are a number of important questions such as that of the *de jure* authority of scripture, the legitimacy of its authority, and its relation to other sources and criteria for doctrine and theology. Such questions can be dealt with adequately only in connection with a genuinely theological account of the character and function of scripture—that is, a critically developed account of how God is involved with scripture, and with us through scripture. The present essay, then, is far from a systematic proposal concerning the authority of scripture for the church or for Christian theology, but it may contribute something, in one way or another, to the development of such a proposal.

6

THEOLOGICAL EDUCATION: Confessional and Public

IN THE FOLLOWING pages, I would like to pursue two main questions. First, how should theological education be conceived? Second, how should the "confessional" and the "public" character of theological education be understood, distinguished, and related?

I. "THEOLOGICAL EDUCATION"

My reflections on the first of these questions come in three parts. First, I will summarize what I take to be the leading developments in the study of theological study in North America in recent years. Second, to illustrate those developments more concretely, I will sketch out my own constructive proposal for the conduct of theological study and theological education. And third, I will briefly suggest some implications of this line of thinking for the concrete practices of teaching, learning, and curricular planning in theological schools.

The Recent Discussion

What knowledge I have of the study of theological study itself arises mainly out of my involvement for a dozen years or so in the "Issues Research Program" of the Association of Theological Schools in the United States and Canada. From the early 1980s into the mid-1990s, this program brought a good many people in North American theological schools into an ongoing conversation about theological education. Those involved in the conversation produced a fair number of publications concerning the aims of theological study and theological education, the ways these enterprises might be restructured so as better to realize those aims, the contexts in which these enterprises are carried on, the training of people to carry them on, and so forth.[1] Some of this research has spurred subsequent studies of theological education in particular ecclesial traditions, and of the graduate education of theological faculties. It has affected curricular design to some extent at a number of theological schools. It has also informed the redevelopment of the standards for accreditation in the Association of Theological Schools (ATS).

In a review of this program of research on basic issues as it was coming to fruition, David Kelsey and Barbara Wheeler identified three points at which the reflections it was producing challenged conventional assumptions about these enterprises—assumptions that have governed our discourse and our practice for a very long time. These points have to do

---

1. See Gilpin, "Basic Issues in Theological Education," on the literature produced in connection with this program in its early years. David H. Kelsey has provided a thorough discussion at a somewhat later stage in his *Between Athens and Berlin*.

with the *goal*, the *movement*, and the *structure* of theological study.²

First, as to the overarching *goal* or *aim* of theological education: The conventional view is that the purpose of theological education is to prepare people for what we Methodists used to call "full-time Christian service"—that is, for employment as pastors, chaplains, directors of religious education, and the like, with the ordained pastor in charge of a congregation or parish more or less as the norm. Theological education is what equips people to do that job; and if decisions are to be made about the content and conduct of theological education, the criterion by which these decisions are made is that of effective preparation for this kind of work. The terms "theological education," "ministerial education," and "education for church leadership" are thus all taken to be nearly synonymous.

The challenge to this conventional view in the recent work on theological education has not usually taken the form of outright rejection. As Kelsey and Wheeler observe, its critics are not "opposed to competence in the clergy";³ further, they are generally agreed that theological study has something to do with that competence. What they oppose is the simple identification of theological education with education for church leadership—an identification that implies, on the one hand, that what unifies the various branches or aspects of theological study is their common orientation to that goal, and, on the other hand, that whatever education seems to prepare persons for church leadership is *ipso facto* theological education. Rather than identify the two in this

2. Kelsey and Wheeler, "Thinking About Theological Education."
3. Ibid., 17.

way, many of us involved in the current discussion want to distinguish them.

Now, to distinguish is not necessarily to separate; it can also be to relate. The question of the relationship of theological study to education for ministry or for church leadership is, then, another item on the agenda of this research.[4] The answer to this question will depend on what alternative view of the overarching goal of theological education is put forth. While there is something of an emerging consensus on this point, namely, that the goal is the development of a particular kind of competence, there are also some significant differences of judgment as to just what kind, and what it is a competence for. Both the emerging consensus and some of the nuances of difference within it are represented handily in a paragraph from the new ATS standards of accreditation, on "Goals of the Theological Curriculum":

> The theological curriculum is the means by which teaching and learning are formally ordered to educational goals. . . . In a theological school, the over-arching goal is the development of theological understanding, that is, aptitude for theological reflection and wisdom pertaining to responsible life in faith. Comprehended in this over-arching goal are others such as deepening spiritual awareness, growing in moral sensibility and character, gaining an intellectual grasp of the tradition of a faith community, and acquiring the abilities requisite to the exercise of ministry in that community. These goals, and the processes leading to their at-

---

4. For one approach, see the first two chapters of my *Invitation to Theological Study*.

> tainment, are normally intimately interwoven and
> should not be separated from one another.[5]

The final sentence of the paragraph just quoted touches on what Kelsey and Wheeler called the second point of challenge in the newer work on theological study, a point having to do with the basic *movement* of theological education, or the dynamics of the process. Recent writers have challenged the conventional and deeply-rooted notion that theological education is a movement from theory to practice. Indeed, some have challenged the very terms in which this issue is normally discussed: "theory" and "practice," the "theoretical" (or sometimes the "classical") disciplines and the "practical" disciplines, the problem of "applying" theory to practice, of "bridging the gap" between them, or of "integrating" the theoretical and the practical aspects. Here, this research draws upon a variety of resources in contemporary philosophy, psychology, educational study, and other fields, but perhaps most of all upon decades of collective experience with curriculum reviews and faculty discussions in which framing the problem in terms of "theory" and "practice" has gotten us exactly nowhere.

What is to take the place of "theory and practice" is, again, a matter of only partial consensus in the recent literature. The consensus, as I read it, is on two points. One is that the theory-to-practice model must be replaced by some model that recognizes the way experience and conduct rightly inform thinking, and not merely the way thinking informs experience and conduct. The other is that, insofar as theological education works, it works not so much by equipping the

5. *Bulletin of the Association of Theological Schools*, 40.

learner with a new theory, that is, with a new interpretation of reality to be applied to practice, as by bringing about a deeper change: by equipping the learner with new ways of perceiving, new abilities, even new dispositions. The desired outcome is not merely a better, more adequate "understanding" of things, but rather a set of new or improved *capacities for* understanding, and for responding to what is understood. This applies as much to, say, biblical studies as it does to pastoral care. In consequence, the neat division of curricular areas into the "academic" and the "practical," into those which impart "knowledge," on the one hand, and those which (merely) impart "skills," on the other, is seen as a very dubious affair, dangerously reductive on both sides. Even the distinction between theological education and personal or spiritual formation, important and valid as it is, needs some new sorting out.[6] When it comes to the constructive articulation of these two points of consensus—the development of alternatives to the theory-to-practice model, and the development of a more adequate account of what theological teaching and learning must involve—the current proposals are varied.

Third, as to the *structure* of theological study: There is a nearly unanimous judgment in the recent literature that the traditional "fourfold curriculum" of biblical, historical, systematic, and practical studies has long outlived whatever rationale it may once have enjoyed, and serves us ill. It originated in the immediate post-Reformation era, and rested on assumptions of various sorts that were severely weakened already by the beginning of the eighteenth century. It was re-engineered then in an uneasy compromise between the church

---

6. See "'Spiritual Formation' and 'Theological Education,'" chapter 3 of my *Invitation to Theological Study*.

and the emerging modern university. It persists today mainly for sociological and political reasons having to do with the traditions of scholarship and of the accreditation of scholarship in the various areas, with the formation of "disciplines" and "professions" in modern culture, with the complex relationships among seminary, university, and church, and with the inertia of ingrained habits of discourse and patterns of association. Its original rationale was largely dependent upon the conventional assumption about the overall aim of theological study (i.e., the preparation of pastoral leadership), and it has also been tied very closely with the conventional assumption about the movement of theological study (i.e., from theory to practice). It is a structure very difficult to shake, even with the best of wills and intentions. When we turn from the observation that the fourfold pattern is problematic to the envisioning of alternatives to it, again we find a variety of proposals, ranging from the rearrangement and reinvigoration of existing disciplines, through their replacement with a different array of disciplines, to the abolition of disciplines altogether (a sort of utopian fantasy, but, like other such fantasies, potentially useful).

A Sample Proposal

My own proposal for addressing all these issues was worked out most systematically (if still sketchily) in a book entitled *Vision and Discernment: An Orientation in Theological Study* (Scholars Press, 1985). A fairly early product of the "issues research" program, this book offers some ideas as to how we might conceive of the goal, movement, and structure of theological study and of theological education. Reviewing these ideas briefly might indicate with a little more specificity how the three challenges just mentioned might be constructively met.

The *goal* of theological education is best conceived, in my judgment, as the fostering of an aptitude for theological reflection. In order for that assertion to be at all informative, I need to explain what I mean by "theological reflection" and what is involved in acquiring and possessing an aptitude for it.

Christian theological reflection may be defined as critical inquiry into the validity of Christian witness. Theological reflection is thus the "second-order" activity of examining and making some judgments about a prior, ongoing "first-order" activity or way of life, namely, the life and work of the Christian community. To call that first-order phenomenon "Christian witness" is somewhat problematic; that designation has its uses, but also its limitations. One might speak instead of "Christian tradition," or "the church's proclamation of the Gospel," or simply "the church." Different Christian communities will have different preferences as to the best way to designate what David Kelsey, following G. K. Chesterton, calls simply "the Christian thing." In any case, the subject matter of theological reflection is some attempt at being Christian. The judgments reached in reflecting upon that attempt may be retrospective (e.g., assessing the practice of some Christian community or individual in the past) or prospective (e.g., trying to determine what one, or one's community, ought to be and to do to carry out the Christian witness, and weighing the merits of various possibilities).

To possess an aptitude for such reflection is both to have an ability for it, and to be disposed to exercise that ability under the appropriate circumstances. Neither the ability nor the disposition by itself is sufficient, which is why theological education must engage both head and heart. It must not only teach students how to think theologically but also persuade them that it is a good and needful thing to do so. For most of the students in our theological schools, this means enabling them to understand and to affirm what theological reflection has to do with the vocations in church leadership for which they are preparing. A large part of the work of theological education is done, or undone, at just that point.

This brings us to the question of the *movement* of theological study and theological education. If the connection just mentioned between theology and ministry is framed in terms of the application of theological theory to the practice of ministry, theological education will be quite predictably undone. The alternative that I would advocate is to think of theological education as a process of reflection, under supervision, on the church's life and work: a process of learning to form judgments by forming judgments, and then thinking about both the judgments and the process by which one arrived at them in the company of someone with perhaps a little more competence, who can provide some suggestions as to what went wrong and how to do better next time.

This supervised reflection on what is going on in the church's life and work gradually produces and refines a capacity for judgment that operates through a constant movement between two poles, or perhaps two mental modes, that I have called "vision" and "discernment." Vision is a capacity for synthesis, for seeing the big picture and making connections; discernment is a capacity for analysis, for noticing what is distinctive about a given situation or problem so that it can be addressed in its specificity. Perhaps the most serious gap in most thinking about theological education, at least in the mainline Protestant tradition, is a general neglect of discernment as something that can and must be taught and learned. What I mean by "discernment" here—and it is well to note that the term can be used in a variety of ways—is a teachable and learnable capacity for analysis, for noticing relevant differences. (If "vision" is a workable rendition of the Greek *theoria*, perhaps "discernment" translates *eisthesis*, the "seeing into" of Philippians 1:9 or Hebrews 5:14.) It seems to me that our conventional way of talking about moving from "theory"—the big picture—to "practice" reflects and encourages a neglect of this aspect of theological education. The movement of theological education, just like the movement of theological reflection itself, is best conceived as a reciprocal process in which both vision and discernment are used and, by that use, constantly strengthened and deepened.

But how is discernment taught and learned? How might the theological curriculum engender in students both vision and discernment as modes of theological judgment? We might draw some helpful analogies from examples of excellence in other disciplines.

In her biography of the Nobel Prize-winning biologist Barbara McClintock, Evelyn Fox Keller calls her "a virtuoso at reading the intricate secrets of maize genetics,"[7] with a remarkable sensitivity to the smallest details. McClintock worked hard to cultivate what she called "a feeling for the

---

7. Keller, *A Feeling for the Organism*, 67–68. I am indebted to an unpublished paper by Charles Bennison for this and subsequent references, and for calling attention to the relevance of McClintock's work to theological education.

organism."[8] When a colleague said "I've often marveled that you can look at a cell under the microscope and see so much," McClintock replied, "Well, you know, when I look at a cell, I get down in that cell and look around."[9] Acquiring that capacity for seeing into things in all their uniqueness requires a kind of self-forgetfulness, and a willingness to allow the material to disclose itself.

Take another example from another field where virtuosity depends on the cultivation of discernment: Learning to play a musical instrument is not just a matter of learning how to do certain things to the instrument to make it produce the effects you want. It is also, and largely, a matter of being taught by the instrument: being willing to allow it to do things to you, letting it show you what you and it together might do. You are not solely agent in that discipline, you are also patient; you are affected, changed. And it is not the case that "when you've played one violin you've played them all." A good musician acquires a capacity to learn from each instrument what its own character is, and to adapt to that character so as to bring out what this particular partnership of instrument and musician can achieve.

What might these examples have to do with theological education? At a fairly concrete level, they suggest the importance of providing, in the context of the curriculum, opportunities for students to *learn from* particular instances of human and Christian experience and practice, as well as opportunities to *learn about* them in a more synoptic fashion. Developing exegetical skills through practice with particular texts, developing a sensitivity to the nuances of human interaction by

8. Ibid., 101.
9. Ibid., 69.

working through case studies of social conflict or of pastoral conversation, acquiring a feeling for the "depth grammar" of Christian doctrine by observing how doctrines structure the life of a Christian community over time, or how they shape individual Christian lives—instances such as these point to the importance of plentiful provision for "inductive" learning and for painstaking attention to particular cases throughout the curriculum. It is precisely through such respect for particularity, combined with resources of a more "theoretical" sort that will help students to see connections and to see things whole, that both discernment and vision may be cultivated.

What does this imply for the *structure* of theological study and learning? First of all, it implies a discarding of the conventional division between theoretical and practical disciplines or areas of the curriculum, or between "knowledge" courses and "skills" courses. Second, it implies a reordering of the disciplinary and curricular structure in a way that will better serve the aim of the endeavor. My own proposal for this (probably nearer to utopian fantasy than to sober expectation) involves a restructuring of theological inquiry and of theological education governed by a consideration of what reflection on the *validity* of Christian witness involves. As I see it, the question of validity when it comes to the performance of what is intended as Christian witness has three components. There is the question of the *authenticity* of the performance of witness: of whether it really represents what it claims to represent, the gospel of Jesus Christ. There is the question of its *intelligibility and truth*: of whether the message embodied therein is, as its proponents say it is, true and worthy of acceptance. And there is the question of whether Christian witness is (or was, or will be) *fittingly enacted* in this instance—that is, of whether the gospel is being related to the specific situation of proclamation in such a way that the truth and life it represents might actually be heard or felt and accepted.

I have gone so far as to project some imaginary theological disciplines corresponding to these three dimensions of theological inquiry. "Historical theology" is the name I have proposed for the discipline that pursues the question of authenticity, that is, of the fidelity of the Christian tradition(s) to the apostolic witness. "Philosophical theology" designates, in my scheme, the discipline devoted to the question of the logic or intelligibility and truth of Christian witness. "Practical theology," long a name for a multiplicity of studies having to do with the tasks of church leadership, I propose to reassign to the discipline that inquires into the fittingness of Christian *praxis* to its context. None of these three disciplines can be rightly pursued in isolation from the others; each requires the others. I think of "systematic theology" as the effort to think these three together. Other theological disciplines or specialties—moral theology, pastoral theology, and so forth—can be viewed as concentrating upon certain aspects or features of Christian witness, for certain purposes. Like other disciplines of study, theological disciplines are cultural artifacts, subject to many adaptations and redefinitions. But the process of change is often subtle, and rarely responsive to deliberate direction. I very much doubt that my proposed disciplinary rearrangement will be embraced by anyone very soon. (And I console myself with the thought that the eminent theologian Friedrich Schleiermacher's proposal for the reform of theological study met with no success in his lifetime.)[10]

10. The formal structure of my threefold scheme is more akin to Barth's than to Schleiermacher's. Barth identifies three main questions theology has to raise about the church's talk about God: Does it *derive*

Some Implications

What might this newer understanding of theological study imply for the concrete practices of teaching, learning, and curricular planning in actual theological schools today? Let me suggest just three lines of thought that might be pursued:

1. It might help us think about how what we who are teachers in theological schools do in our particular courses and fields might relate to the overarching aim of the theological curriculum. Rather than taking our cues only from the inner identity and trajectory of our specific disciplines, we might think about the aims of our teaching in relation to some common aims in theological study.

2. It might also help us think, in light of the aims of our teaching, about *how* to do what we do: about both the pedagogy and the content of our courses.

3. It might help us into conversation as colleagues in a theological school about ways of understanding and realizing our aims together. Without this kind of conversation, discussions of curriculum revision quickly degenerate into battles over territory. The battling might be mitigated if we had some better sense of perspective than we are likely to have if all we can think about is what a student needs to know about whatever it is we ourselves teach.

---

from Jesus Christ? Does it *lead to* him? Is it *in accord with* him? For Barth, these are all interdependent components of the one question about the truth, and Jesus Christ is the criterion of the truth. See Barth, *Church Dogmatics* I/1:4–5. I have utilized Barth's scheme more directly in Wood and Blue, *Attentive to God*, esp. 9–12.

II. "CONFESSIONAL AND PUBLIC"

How should the "confessional" and the "public" character of theological education be understood, distinguished, and related? In the way this question is stated, and in the way the statement is anticipated in the title of this paper, a thesis is implicit: theological education is to be conceived as confessional *and* public. Often, at least in the settings with which I am most familiar, the relationship is assumed to be disjunctive: theology and theological education can be either confessional or public, perhaps, but certainly not both—or at least, not both at the same time.

Here I want to explicate and defend the thesis that good theology and good theological education are always *both* confessional and public. In order to do so, I will need to do several things. Accordingly, my reflections have three parts. First, I will briefly examine some ways of construing the meaning of "confessional" and "public" that would suggest a disjunctive relationship between them. Then I will explore at somewhat more length the possibility of a "conjunctive" understanding. Third and finally, I will ask what this understanding might imply for the practice of theological education in a variety of specific settings.

Confessional or *Public*

When we refer to theological education as "confessional" or "public," what might we mean by those terms? Although in a specific context it may be obvious to everyone just what is meant, in the broader discussion of theological education these adjectives are used in a variety of ways, and so it may be worthwhile to mention some possible senses. These are not mutually exclusive alternatives; the connotations can easily overlap. Still, there are some significant principles of distinction that can be brought out. Let us look first at some ways of interpreting "confessional" and "public" as disjunctive terms. I will mention four of these—surely not an exhaustive list.

First, when we refer to "confessional" and "public" theological education, we may be referring simply to two different ways theological education may be established and financed. We might thus define a "confessional" curriculum as one that has ecclesiastical sponsorship and support, while a "public" curriculum is one that operates under state or government auspices, with public funding. In either case, various expectations may accompany the provision of support; money is rarely free. But we might decide to use the terms in this way, i.e., to make the source of support the determining factor in whether to call an institution or program confessional or public.

Another way we might distinguish between "confessional" and "public" theological education would be to say that a confessional program confines its attention to one religious tradition, while a public program studies a variety of religious traditions. In this case, it is not the source of support, but rather the scope of the subject matter, that determines whether a curriculum is confessional or public.

A third way of stipulating the distinction between confessional and public theological education would be to say that a confessional curriculum serves what we might call religious interests—aiming, for example, to help its students grow spiritually, or to prepare them for ministerial leadership—while a public curriculum serves what we might call academic interests, aiming at the understanding of religion but not at its practice.

Finally, a fourth disjunctive way of distinguishing between "confessional" and "public" is this: a "confessional" school (or faculty or curriculum) is one in which certain ideas—normally, ideas important to the identity and interests of the school's sponsoring denomination—are explicitly ruled to be beyond question, while in a "public" setting for theological education such constraints upon inquiry do not apply. A school that is confessional in this way may require its members literally to subscribe a confession, that is, a common declaration of faith or statement of principles, and to promise, as a condition of their membership in the school, that they will not teach or advocate anything inconsistent with that statement. There may be a more positive counterpart to this expectation, namely, that the members *will* teach and advocate what the confession sets forth. A school of this sort may have some explicit procedures for enforcing doctrinal discipline and dealing with infractions, either directly or in cooperation with the authorities of the sponsoring church. Of course, a school may be "confessional" in this sense even where there is no formal act of subscription and no formal procedures for monitoring members' compliance, but where there is a clear (if unwritten) understanding that certain teachings and practices will be upheld and certain questions are not to be asked. Similarly, a school may *not* be confessional in this sense even if it requires a formal act of subscription, if the act is understood to mean something different—if, for instance (to take an extreme example), everyone regards it as a *pro forma* ritual of admission with no bearing whatsoever on the actual practices of teaching and learning. (A school that is formally confessional but has become functionally nonconfessional in this sense may find itself in an awkward situation if for some reason the dormant confessional expectations are later revived and enforced.)

Advocates of a confessional approach to theological education in this fourth sense are often quite clear about the antithetical relationship between "confessional" and "public" that it implies. For example, R. Albert Mohler, Jr., the current president of Southern Baptist Theological Seminary in Louisville, Kentucky, has written in a defense of "confessionalism" that

> we now face a landscape with two opposing cultures of theological education. The confessional culture understands its primary public of accountability to be the churches. The nonconfessional culture sees its primary public as the academy. The issue comes down to this: Who sets the norms and establishes final accountability? Evangelical institutions must stand ready to declare their theological convictions and maintain unapologetic fidelity to their confessions and churches. . . . [T]heological education severed from confessional accountability is immediately vulnerable to the accommodationist pressures of modern secular culture.[11]

Although Mohler does not use the word "public" as the alternative to "confessional," the disjunction is clear; and in this case, what is determinative is accountability. The theological school that is "nonconfessional" is captive to the norms of the modern, secular academy. "Confessionalism must be guarded by sustained relationships with identifiable churches, who hold the seminary accountable."[12] For Mohler, the proper

11. Mohler, "Thinking of the Future," 279–80.

12. Ibid., 280. The sort of accountability Mohler has in mind is illustrated by the recent history of the Southern Baptist seminaries in

home of confessional theological education is the church-owned seminary, under the church's ever-watchful eye.

The understanding of theology and of theological education that Mohler advocates is radically different from the understanding I proposed in the first part of this paper. If Christian theology is a critical inquiry into the validity of particular ways of being Christian or of bearing Christian witness, and if theological education aims at the cultivation of an aptitude for theological reflection, it is difficult to imagine how either one could flourish in the atmosphere of this sort of "confessionalism." It is worth noting that, when ATS voted to adopt its current standards for accreditation in June of 1996, Mohler's seminary and a handful of other Southern Baptist schools committed to similar principles were the only ATS member institutions that refused to vote in the affirmative. Mohler and his colleagues might construe the new standards as evidence of the capitulation of the ATS to the spirit of the secular academy. Others, myself included, see these standards as deeply rooted in the spirit of Christian confession. But to see them thus is to have a different understanding of the confessional character of Christian faith and of Christian theology and theological education from the one informing Mohler's prescriptions. Another evangelical scholar, Gabriel Fackre, writing in the same volume that contains Mohler's essay, might have been responding directly to Mohler's view when he wrote: "A faithful seminary is not, finally, accountable to its ecclesiastical tribe, but only to its Lord. Indeed, just

---

the United States. Several of these schools have been in difficulty with the accrediting agencies because of the way fundamentalist forces in the Southern Baptist Convention have enforced "orthodoxy" within the schools.

as the discipline of theology is said to be the self-scrutiny of the church's preaching and teaching, so the theological school, at best, is the church's loving critic-in-residence."[13] It is time to look at an understanding of the confessional and public character of theological education in keeping with this vision of our accountability.

Confessional and *Public*

For some help with this, I want to turn to the account of the confessional character of theology found in H. Richard Niebuhr's *The Meaning of Revelation*, written some sixty years ago. Niebuhr's thought had considerable influence on the reshaping of Protestant theological education in North America in the latter half of the twentieth century, owing in part to his leadership in a major study of theological education in the late 1950s, and in part to his influence, as a teacher and as a thinker, on several generations of theologians.

Niebuhr's emphasis on the constant necessity of intellectual repentance is a leading mark of his thought. In the preface to *The Meaning of Revelation*, he stated three guiding convictions:

> The first is the conviction that self-defense is the most prevalent source of error in all thinking and perhaps especially in theology and ethics. . . . The second idea is that the great source of evil in life is the absolutizing of the relative, which in Christianity takes the form of substituting religion, revelation, church or Christian morality for God. The third conviction . . . is that Christianity is "permanent

---

13. Fackre, "Educating the Church," 276.

revolution," or *metanoia* which does not come to
an end in this world, this life, or this time.[14]

For Niebuhr, "all knowledge is conditioned by the standpoint of the knower."[15] Our standpoint both enables us to know whatever it is that we know, and limits our knowledge. All communication of knowledge is a matter of telling someone else how things appear to us from our point of view. This is no less true in Christian faith and theology than in other realms. Christian proclamation and teaching, thus understood, are inevitably confessional, both in that they involves a declaration of what our standpoint and our particular relation to the subject-matter have allowed us to see, and in that they require an owning up to the limitations and the self-interest that have affected our knowing. "[W]e can proceed," Niebuhr says, "only by stating in simple, confessional form what has happened to us in our community, how we came to believe, how we reason about things and what we see from our point of view."[16] To be "confessional" in this sense is quite different from espousing unquestionable truths. It is rather a matter of sharing what one has come to see, and giving an account of how one has come to see it.

This understanding of the necessarily confessional character of proclamation and teaching goes hand in hand with a commitment to their public character. When we learn to "confess" what we see from our point of view, we no longer pretend that our knowledge is infallible or immune from scrutiny. (Niebuhr remarked: "It was said of a German phi-

14. Niebuhr, *Meaning of Revelation*, x.
15. Ibid., 5.
16. Ibid., 29.

losopher of religion that he regarded as innate truths of reason all the ideas he had learned before he was five years old; the statement is more or less applicable to all men."[17]) Implicitly or explicitly, to confess is to invite correction. We offer our understanding as a contribution to a wider conversation. Our conversation partners, hearing us out, may come to share our point of view and to see things as we do, or they may offer an alternative account of things from their own point of view that attracts us to such an extent that we experience a conversion. More likely than either of these outcomes is one in which both we and they find our own views in some respects challenged, in some respects confirmed, and in some respects amplified by means of the encounter. "To see ourselves as others see us, or to have others communicate to us what they see when they regard our lives from the outside is to have a moral experience," Niebuhr observed.[18] In any case, what this understanding of the meaning of "confession" rules out is the possibility of exempting one's beliefs from critical discussion. Rather than cutting off critical inquiry, confession invites it. This is the posture of "faith seeking understanding."

What does such a conception of the confessional and the public aspects of Christian witness imply for theological education? In order to explore that question we need to take a look at some of the places where theological education happens.

17. Ibid., 11.
18. Ibid., 62.

Contexts of Theological Education

In observing the North American discussion of theological education for several years, David Kelsey noticed something odd about it. The discussion tended to remain at an abstract level. Those of us involved in it normally spoke in generalities about the aims and purposes of theological education; we rarely spoke about theological schools, about actual institutions and programs and what went on in them. Kelsey rightly saw this as a serious limitation. In his own major contribution to the literature, published in 1992, he wrote:

> "Education" is a very abstract term. It is used to designate a process. But the educational process always takes place in some particular institutional setting located in a particular socioeconomic context, has a particular ethos of its own that amounts to a "culture" open to ethnographic study, has its own structure of power, is offered by a particular group of faculty members themselves socialized in various ways as academic professionals, and is undergone by a particular student body. The phrase "theological education" misleadingly invites us to consider our topic in abstraction from much or all of that.[19]

What happens if, instead of talking about the aims and character of theological education, we talk about the aims and character of the theological school? This is the question Kelsey set out to investigate. Immediately he discovered that it is impossible to talk about "the theological school"; one must instead talk about different sorts of theological schools. Theological schooling is pluralistic. Among the "pluralizing

19. Kelsey, *To Understand God Truly*, 16–17.

factors," as he calls them, are the ways different schools are situated in relation to the church and the academy, and the particular churchly and academic traditions to which they are related. Although Kelsey chose the term "school" to represent the institutional embodiment of theological education, he would surely recognize that not all theological education goes on in schools of theology. His observations are applicable, *mutatis mutandis*, to theological programs and curricula in other institutional settings, for example, in colleges and universities.

Given the plurality of contexts and specific forms of theological education, does the concept itself have any coherence? The differences between theological teaching in a small church-related seminary and in a university department of religious studies may be so prominent as to obscure any common features, particularly if the inhabitants of each context have reason to exaggerate those differences in their own favor.

When one moves from the level of abstract and polemical declarations of principle to the level of actual practice, a different picture emerges. A few years ago, I participated in a consultation of scholars representing the leading doctoral programs in which members of the theological faculties in North America receive their graduate training. These are also among the leading programs educating faculty members for college and university departments of religious studies. The subject of the consultation was the future shape of graduate education for theological faculties.[20] We considered ques-

20. The report of the consultation, "The Doctoral Education of Theological Faculties," is available from the Auburn Center for the Study of Theological Education, Auburn Theological Seminary, New York.

tions such as: How should prospective teachers and scholars in theological schools be prepared for the kind of teaching and the kind of scholarship that will be expected of them in that context? What are the problems with our current graduate programs in this regard, and how might these problems be addressed? Are there any significant differences between the kind of education that best prepares one for teaching in a theological context (for example, in a seminary or department of theology) and the kind that best prepares one for teaching in a religious studies context (for example, a university department or program of religious studies)?

After several meetings in which we discussed (among many other things) how theological studies and religious studies might best be distinguished, we put aside those abstract issues temporarily and got into a discussion about teaching: that is, about what we, as teachers, actually do, and why. We gradually discovered that, regardless of the level of the teaching we were engaged in (undergraduate, graduate-professional, or doctoral) and regardless of whether the context was primarily that of theological education or that of religious studies, our pedagogical aims were remarkably similar. Further reflection on this discussion has led me to identify three aims we seemed to hold in common. I do not recall that we ever considered all three together or wondered how they might relate, although some sorts of relations may appear obvious. These are not conflicting aims. All three might be pursued within the same program or course of study, or even within the same course.

One aim is to bring students to a basic grasp of the content of a religious tradition or traditions. The emphasis may be upon the tradition as a whole, or upon some particular part or aspect of it (for example, its doctrines, rituals, or organization). In any case, the aim is to enable students to gain some sort of thematized understanding of it. Whether the religious tradition is the students' own or another, the understanding sought here may rightly be described as to some extent personal, holistic, self-involving or existential, rather than merely rational and intellectual.

A second aim is to develop in the students some ability to analyze and to reflect responsibly and critically upon various elements of the religious tradition or traditions they are coming to understand; to foster a capacity for reasoned judgment as to (for example) the intelligibility, consistency, significance, and cogency of the claims, values, and practices embodied in these traditions.

A third aim might be called a transformative one. It is to enable students to incorporate the understanding and the judgments they have reached in their study of the religious tradition(s) into their own life-practice—a process which also extends and deepens their understanding and reflective judgment. Indeed, all three aims and the practices leading to their achievement are closely related and mutually reinforcing.

A Luther specialist overhearing our discussion on that day might have recognized in this emerging articulation of three aims the pattern of *oratio*, *meditatio*, and *tentatio*—of receptivity, reflection, and response—that Martin Luther commended as the basic structure of theological study.[21] While the comparison might come as a shock to some of those scholars in religious studies who wish to maintain a sharp distinction between religious studies and theological studies, the evidence seems clear in practice. A single undergraduate-

21. *D. Martin Luthers Werke*, 50:658–61.

level introductory course in religion will not, of course, be likely to get as far toward the realization of any of these aims as several years of immersion in the study of a single tradition (and in either case, the approaches taken may hinder rather than further students' progress in actually achieving the abilities aimed at), but the aims themselves appear to be widely shared. Any or all three of them may characterize any given program in the field, e.g., in an undergraduate religious studies or theology department, a graduate department, or the various programs of a theological school. Neat distinctions, then, between the aims of undergraduate and graduate programs, academic and professional programs, seminary and university programs, or religious studies and theology programs, would seem to have great difficulty standing the test of practice, at least at present.

At the same time, those associated with a given program may justifiably give prominence to some version of one or another of these aims and think of it as *the* aim, or the superordinate aim, of their program, or even of the overall enterprise to which that program belongs when rightly conceived. The ideal embodied in the ATS standards that the "over-arching goal" of a theological school's curriculum should be "the development of theological understanding, that is, aptitude for theological reflection and wisdom pertaining to responsible life in faith," and that other legitimate aims should be seen in relationship to that overarching goal, represents one such decision about priorities. A proposal about the "overarching goal" of instruction in religious studies or theology in the context of the liberal arts might look quite different from this one, while still featuring, in some combination, the three basic ingredients of understanding, reflective judgment, and appropriation.

Some academic environments are more hospitable than others to the realization of these aims. A "confessionalist" school in Mohler's sense is probably among the less hospitable. At the other extreme, an academic ethos that is hostile to religion or is in the grip of an uncritical allegiance to Enlightenment rationalism may be equally inhospitable. However, it should be acknowledged that these are both extreme cases. It is increasingly recognized in the academy that all teaching and learning is "confessional," in something like Niebuhr's sense. An acknowledgement that there is no "standpointless" inquiry, and no fully disinterested inquiry, and thus no standpointless or disinterested teaching and learning, has come to pervade higher education across most disciplines. Complementing this—as the example of Barbara McClintock may suggest—has been a growing recognition of the importance of a personal "engagement" with the subject matter, as distinct from an artificial objectification of it. It may turn out in the long run that some key principles in theological education are in fact key principles in any significant field of learning.

My late colleague John Deschner, a student of both H. Richard Niebuhr and Karl Barth who gave much service to the ecumenical movement, was my teaching partner in a team-taught course in systematic theology for many years until his retirement in 1991. While I was developing and presenting in our classes my understanding of Christian theology as "a critical inquiry into the validity of Christian witness," and was constantly stressing the need for a rigorously critical approach, my colleague worked out in response his own definition of theology. The church's theological task, as he stated it, was "to explicate and thus to test the truth of its own service of God in our contemporary situation." He agreed with me that the basic theological task was criticism, but he insisted that theology should be, as he put it, "constructive in form, though critical in aim."[22]

In recent years I have found myself appreciating the wisdom of his approach more and more. "To explicate, and thus to test": that is, I think, an apt summary of an approach to theology and to theological education that is both genuinely confessional and genuinely public.

---

22. These quotations are from my notes on his class lectures in the mid-1980s.

7

NOT EVERY SCHOOL

SEVERAL YEARS AGO, Christopher Morse, a theologian who teaches at Union Theological Seminary in New York City, published what he called "a dogmatics of Christian disbelief." Its title is *Not Every Spirit*. The title is taken from 1 John 4:1: "Beloved, do not believe every spirit, but test the spirits to see whether they are from God; for many false prophets have gone out into the world." Morse begins from the premise that "to believe in God is not to believe everything." Faith in God requires *dis*believing a great deal. Some of that "faithful disbelieving," as Morse calls it, takes no great effort. Some beliefs hardly tempt us. On the other hand, some faithful disbelieving takes a lot of effort, because what we should be disbelieving is deeply ingrained in us, or taken for granted in our culture, or embedded in our own religious tradition (tradition is always a mixture of faith and what faith struggles against). For Morse, one of the best ways for the faithful community to clarify its faith is to articulate its disbeliefs. What are we obliged to reject for the sake of what we hold? What is the "no" that accompanies the "yes" of faith?[1]

This question is not answered simply by pronouncing anathemas against old heresies, and affirming old, accepted formulations. The old formulations may harbor error, and each new situation may proffer fresh ways of confusing faith with its opposite. The investigation must be constantly renewed. Like earlier advocates of the same approach to Christian confession, and noting such more recent exemplars as the signers of the Barmen Declaration in Nazi Germany and the authors of the Kairos Document in South Africa, Morse advises us to pay attention to how faith in God is presently under attack, whether blatantly or subtly, and to discern what each new situation obliges us to disbelieve, in order to arrive at a fresh understanding and more apt enactment of our genuine commitments.

This sort of clarifying exercise can be extremely valuable. The general approach has value beyond the context of a systematic clarification of Christian or other religious belief, however. Here I want to suggest its applicability to a more specific subject, namely, the enterprise in which theological schools or seminaries are engaged. Just as it is important to keep in mind that not every candidate for our believing is consistent with faith in God ("not every spirit is from God"), so it may be well to consider the possibility that not everything that would like to go by the name of theological education really is theological education. It is at least conceivable that not every school presenting itself as a theological school really is a theological school.

---

1. Morse, *Not Every Spirit: A Dogmatics of Christian Disbelief*, 6–13.

Now, the main reason we should give this possibility some thought is not so that we might point at those "other" schools out there, near and far, which by our lights are clearly not theological schools, which are clearly operating under false pretenses, and then to glory in our own righteousness; rather, as you may suspect, the idea is to prompt some self-examination. For faith nurtured by the biblical traditions, the false beliefs we most need to worry about are not those false beliefs over there in our neighbors—the ones that are easy to label and that present no particular temptation to us—but these false beliefs right here in our own hearts. Just so, the theological schooling whose credentials we most need to worry about is the theological schooling for which we bear some direct responsibility and in which we ourselves are invested; and the dangers we need to be concerned about are the ones we are least inclined to recognize as such.

During the 1920s, Rudolf Bultmann offered several courses of lectures on the study of theology to entering theological students in Marburg. These lectures were published a few years ago, and they make interesting reading, not least because Bultmann had some things to say there that may help us into the right sort of worry about what we're doing in our theological schools. He made it clear to those entering theological students that he had no use for "pious theology," and that they shouldn't either. In fact, he said, there is no such thing. What was apparently going by the name of "pious theology," and had gotten Bultmann's attention, was simply the most recent attempt to erase the distinction between Christian theology and Christian proclamation so that theology became an extension of the church's witness rather than (as it should be) a critical examination of that witness.

Theology thus pressed into service as witness (from so-called pious motives) loses its character as theology, for theology exists only as that enterprise of critical inquiry in which the community's proclamation is measured by the standards appropriate to it. The outcome of that inquiry cannot be predetermined, and it may well complicate the church's life in some measure, at least in the short run. For Bultmann, theology serves proclamation by checking up on it. It is a reflective task. The service of theology to proclamation, as he liked to say, can only be an indirect one.[2] "Pious theology" wants to circumvent that reflective task. It wants theology to be engaged in witness directly. It simply begs the theological question, or regards it as already settled, in order to get on with a predetermined agenda.

At the same time that he denied the legitimacy or possibility of "pious theology," Bultmann affirmed that theological inquiry could be—indeed, as he saw it, must be—an act of faith. There should be no pious theology, but there should be pious theologians. Theology is possible, according to Bultmann, only as the work of the faithful individual, the faithful community, reflecting on faith from faith and for faith.[3] It may be well to recall that for Bultmann, "faith" does not mean, in the first instance, the holding of certain beliefs; what is primary and decisive, in this connection as elsewhere, is the existential attitude which Bultmann associated with the traditional term *fiducia*, involving both trust and free response. Faith in this sense is what both requires and permits

---

2. Bultmann, *Theologische Enzyklopädie*, 163–67.

3. Ibid., 163–66. Eberhard Jüngel cites and develops the "from faith to faith" aspect of this understanding in his treatment of Bultmann's *Enzyklopädie*: Jüngel, *Glauben und Verstehen*, 24.

theological inquiry. That is, faith itself demands that "pious theology" be avoided, and that genuine theology be pursued. Genuine theology—rigorous and uncompromising testing of the adequacy of our faith and witness—is itself a faithful act. It is possible only as an act of faith. And yet, as Bultmann saw, it is always in danger of being subverted in the name of faith. What you get then is pious theology. Domesticated theology, you might say. Theology that has been trained to behave. Theology without any teeth or claws. Theology that is not going to create any problems. Theology that will do our bidding. In other words, no theology at all. And sooner or later, what you also get with this arrangement is no authentic faith or authentic witness at all, but something else under those names.

The distinction between theology and witness that Bultmann, among others, has made and defended is crucial to both the theological enterprise and the life and integrity of communities of faith. Christian witness—Christian proclamation and practice—needs the constant testing which genuine theology can give it, if it is to be true to its own aims; but theology can be genuine only so long as its own character as a reflective inquiry is acknowledged and supported—that is, only so long as its distinction from witness as such is properly maintained.

There is, of course, a sense in which the pursuit and encouragement of theological inquiry is itself a testimony of faith as well as an act of faith. As Schubert Ogden has put it, "The existence of radical theological freedom in the church is the clearest evidence it can give of its deep conviction in the abiding truth of its witness."[4] That a religious community

4. Ogden, "Doctrinal Standards in the United Methodist Church," 45.

not only allows but encourages and supports and invests in the ongoing scrutiny of the adequacy of its own faith and practice, and actually teaches not only its leaders but also its members to engage in this sort of critical reflection, can be a powerful testimony to its own faith. It suggests that this community has more confidence in the faithfulness of God than in the correctness of its own understanding or the adequacy of its own response. It suggests that the community is willing to engage in repentance, and sees it as an occasion for renewal of life.

The less welcome counterpart of this thought should also be acknowledged: a religious community that inhibits and discourages theological inquiry, that is disinclined to engage in it or to see others engaged in it, that does its best to prevent it—whether by neglect, or by outright opposition, or by efforts to co-opt and domesticate it—also bears witness. There are all sorts of ways a community may get itself into that attitude and situation, and it is unwise to judge a particular instance without careful investigation of the circumstances. But it is at least worth asking whether a community taking such a position, whether deliberately or otherwise, does not manifest to the world a lack of confidence in the truth (and in the One who is the truth), a preference for its own priorities, an unwillingness to subject its own convictions and practices to examination.

Just a few years after Bultmann's lectures, Karl Barth, in making his own case for an understanding of theology as the ongoing criticism and revision of the church's talk about God in the light of the Word of God, wrote a sentence that has stuck with me since I first read it: "The whole church must seriously want a serious theology if it is to have a serious theology."[5] The evidence of the church's serious intentions was not exactly overwhelming when Barth wrote these words; nor, I am afraid, is it now.

As with serious theology, so with serious theological schooling. The pressures to do something else and call it theological schooling are manifold and unrelenting. Some are external, some are internal. Certainly the health of a theological school, its capacity to be a genuine theological school, is affected by the encouragement or discouragement—or, as is sometimes the case, the ambiguous mixture of both—that it receives from the religious body or bodies to which it is related. The theological health of a school is also affected by the broader academic climate in which it finds itself, and by its social and cultural context. But it is not determined solely by these factors. Some schools maintain their integrity under remarkably adverse circumstances. And some lose their integrity when there is very little external inducement for them to do so.

What we might call "pious theological schooling"—the educational form of Bultmann's "pious theology"—comes in several interesting varieties. Most of them occur when something else takes the place of theological education, while retaining the title. For a long stretch of time, for many theological schools, this something else has been training in the functional specialties of ministerial practice. But there are a number of other contenders. For example, many schools, as well as their sponsoring religious bodies, have lately been struck by the fact that, for various reasons, fewer and fewer entering seminarians bring with them significant, long-term acquaintance with and experience in local congregations, and thus lack much socialization into the religious ethos and tra-

5. Barth, *Church Dogmatics*, I/1:77.

dition. They do not, so to speak, have the raw material upon which theological reflection is supposed to work, nor do they have a well-developed sense of their own religious identity. Consequently, these schools find themselves doing a great deal of what we might call basic religious education, in all its dimensions. Likewise, theological schools are discovering that a good number of their students are dealing with relatively serious emotional or psychic injury, and a therapeutic element in the school's work is increasing in significance. A third important factor at present (certainly not for the first time in our history) is the conviction widely shared by numbers of students and faculty members alike that our religious communities and traditions—and, not least, the theological schools themselves—are in serious need of reform to address long-standing social injustices. An element of advocacy or emancipatory practice has assumed a significant role in the life of many theological schools, alongside or combined with the basic educational and therapeutic elements just mentioned. There are other needs and pressures, and other activities responding to them, that could be cited.

I do not mention these elements in order to exclude them from the rightful purview of a theological school. A case might be made for each one's rightful belonging in a theological school, at least given our present arrangements and circumstances. In the typical North American theological school (if there is such a thing), probably all four of the elements named above should currently figure into what goes on. Ideally, the right sort of attention to them all would enhance the theological education which is the school's central mission. The problem arises not when such elements are introduced into theological education, but rather when any such element, or a combination of them, comes to *replace* theological education—to coopt its resources along with its name, so that theological education never happens. This is a self-defeating move in the long run; nevertheless, it is powerfully tempting.

What seems essential in guarding against this turn of events is some careful work on relating the various things we do in a theological school to the primary aim of theological schooling. As I understand it, theological schooling has as its primary aim the development and exercise of an aptitude for theology: an aptitude for critical and constructive reflection upon a living religious tradition and upon one's own participation in it. When the religious community supports such schooling, and its members engage deliberately in it, it is for the sake of the integrity of the community's faith and life. That is, the development of the aptitude is normally *ordered to* more effective, more faithful, more truthful response to the call of God.

The aptitude for theology is learned as students actually engage in theological reflection, with some guidance and supervision from people who have had more experience at it. The concrete subject matter on which they reflect can vary a great deal, and in fact must vary a great deal if they are to achieve a breadth of competence. For example, a person who wishes to learn to think theologically about the leadership of worship must ordinarily do this in the context of actual worship and its leadership. Growth in proficiency as a leader of worship and growth in the capacity to think theologically about that practice will proceed simultaneously, if all goes well. The same goes for a host of other specific areas. But what is being gained—again, if all goes well—is not just a collection of particular abilities relevant to particular tasks. What is being gained is a more integral, fundamental aptitude for reflection which enables thoughtful attention to whatever particular situation may be before one, as well as an overall grasp of the context to which those particular situations belong.

The question before every theological school is whether, in the attention it gives to the tasks of ministry, or to spiritual formation, or to therapeutic growth, or to issues of social justice, or to scripture, it is helping students to cultivate theological aptitude. Is everything that it does ordered to this objective somehow? Or is its work ordered to some other overall objective it might be able to identify? Or is it simply doing a bunch of things with no particular common purpose?

The question for every school that claims the title is: Is it really a theological school? Or is it a place where a little theology is tolerated so long as it doesn't get in the way of more pressing objectives? Some other questions may lead us to see how this one is being answered in the life of a particular school. Is theological scholarship affirmed as the heart of the school's work? Is it something in which every teacher and learner is engaged? Is the teaching and learning that goes on, in whatever specific area of the curriculum, so conducted as to give priority to the development of the critical and self-critical capacity that theology is? Do the resources—faculty, library, curriculum, space, ethos—permit and encourage a student to develop theological competence? Is the fully critical and self-critical character of theological inquiry and theological education clearly affirmed, and is the school clear about the intellectual and spiritual space that this requires?

In his recent book, *To Understand God Truly: What's Theological about a Theological School*, David H. Kelsey develops an account of the marks of excellence in theological schooling that I find very promising. He frames this account in terms of his own definition of a theological school, which in turn rests upon an understanding of what a school is. Kelsey defines a school as "a particular community of persons whose central purpose is to understand some subject truly." Teaching and learning are "subordinate moments" in the realization of that purpose. "What distinguishes a theological school," Kelsey goes on to propose, "is that the subject it seeks to understand truly is *theos*, God." Since God cannot be studied directly, the community "studies those matters which are believed to *lead* to true understanding of God."[6]

Kelsey suggests that, for theological purposes at least, we understand "understanding" primarily as a matter of conceptual competence; to understand something is to have a particular ability with regard to it. The sorts of abilities to be sought with regard to God are "abilities and capacities that make possible new sorts of *discernment* and *response* regarding God"[7]—capacities to apprehend God's presence, to assess one's life in relation to God, to act in a situation so as to respond to God, and so forth. Acquiring and strengthening this understanding is ordinarily a matter of long-term involvement in linguistically-structured practices through which conceptual and personal growth are interwoven.

The goal of theological schooling to understand God *truly* brings in a serious element of self-critique. In fact, says Kelsey, that goal requires that self-critique be "an institutionalized feature" of all of the school's practices—of its teaching and learning, its use of resources, its governance, and so on.

6. Kelsey, *To Understand God Truly*, 31.
7. Ibid., 168.

He elaborates this point into a statement of "two sets of marks of excellence in theological schooling":

> The first set [of marks of excellence] is this: [A theological school] is excellent to the extent that the conceptual growth [it fosters] is guided by an interest in God for God's own sake. It is excellent to the extent that precisely because it is guided by that interest, it is self-critically concerned with the truthfulness of its discernment and response to God. It is excellent to the extent that precisely because it is guided by interest in God for God's own sake, it honors the inevitable pluralism of understandings of God by serious engagement in conversation with differing understandings. It is excellent to the extent that, precisely because its guiding interest is in God for God's own sake, it is self-critical of ideological distortions of its own efforts to understand God.
>
> A second set of marks of excellence in theological schooling comes into view when we turn to reflect on the *concreteness* of a theological school [Note: one of Kelsey's aims in his book is to see what difference it makes if, instead of talking about theological education in the abstract, we talk about the theological school—a more tangible, concrete entity]: Its concreteness consists in part in its having institutionalized practices of governance, and its schooling is excellent to the extent that its polity leaves room so that the effort to understand God can be genuine by being free to err. Its concreteness in part consists of its transactions with its immediate host community, and its schooling is excellent to the extent that its transactions are deliberately and self-critically shaped in such a way that what they

> symbolize to the immediate neighborhood and what they teach members of the school community itself are consonant with the concepts taught and learned in its central practices. Its concreteness in part consists of its own internal arrangements of power and status, and its schooling is excellent to the extent that built into these institutionalized arrangements are mechanisms fostering ideology critique within the school.[8]

What David Kelsey is offering us in these words, I believe, is a way of thinking holistically about the theological accountability of a theological school to be a sure-enough, genuine theological school: not a place engaged in pious theological schooling, not a place where a little theology is done by a few people in one section of the curriculum, but a place where theological reflection is the hallmark of *everything* that goes on: the school's involvement in the spiritual formation, faith development, and growth toward health of all its participants, its involvement in the religious community and in the wider society, the education for ministry and leadership that it provides, the way teaching and learning happens, its structures and practices of governance, and much more.

There are many things to claim our attention as we think about the fundamental values to be fostered in theological education in the present context. My suggestion here has been that organizing our thinking around the question of the constitutive purpose of a theological school might be a good way to start.

---

8. Ibid., 192.

8

PAYING ATTENTION

"WHAT IS THEOLOGICAL about what you do?" Several years ago, a group of Protestant church leaders from various traditions and backgrounds began an extended consultation on theological education by sharing their reflections on that question. The consultation, a series of meetings over a period of two and a half years, was an effort to bring church leaders into the intensive discussion of basic issues in theological education that had been underway then for a decade, and which up to that point had mainly involved faculty and administrators in theological schools. Like many of the projects in this ongoing study, this consultation was supported by the Lilly Endowment.

These church leaders did not join the discussion as representatives of their denominations or in any other official capacity, but simply as practitioners whose range of abilities and experience in church leadership seemed likely to yield some worthwhile contributions. As someone who has written on theological education, I was invited to their first gathering, mainly to listen and learn. I was then invited back to their final session, and given the task of preparing a synopsis of what transpired. That synopsis, revised and refined somewhat in light of the participants' comments on it, is the substance of this brief essay.

In dealing with that initial question—"What is theological about what you do?"—these practitioners in ministry did not, on the whole, do what many would have expected them to do. They did not identify "theology" with the work of the systematic theologians they had read in seminary or since, and then talk about how those writings had or had not been helpful to them in the practice of ministry. They did not speak of theology as "theory," which had somehow to be related to something called "practice." They did not talk about the difficulty of "integrating" the various disciplines of theological study with each other or with the realm of churchly activity. They did not appear to think in terms of a dichotomy between the "academic" and the "practical."

Instead, their responses to the question indicated that they took "theology" to stand for a way of thinking in which they themselves were constantly engaged. To call it a way of thinking, however, may not quite do justice to the scope and depth of the activity as they described it. It might be more accurate to say that, for these practitioners in ministry, theology is above all *a way of paying attention*: a way of paying attention to God, and to everything else.

Paying attention in this way is evidently a key element in these leaders' own faith and Christian life, inseparable from both prayer and action. It is more or less deliberate and reflective, depending on the circumstances. It is rooted in an aptitude formed and sustained through learning. As evidenced in how they talked about it, that aptitude involves a capacity to read situations, as well as Christian scripture and tradition, theologically. Those readings appear to inform one another to such an extent that they are often difficult to distinguish in practice, and to be ordered to a more profound sort of listening to God through both situations and texts.

In their first meeting, the participants established a good bit of common ground and also identified significant differences of background and approach. Each then accepted the task of writing a substantial paper, informed to whatever extent they found useful by the recent literature on theological education or by whatever else they chose, on some aspect of the general topic. These papers were discussed in subsequent sessions, and reworked in between.

At the final meeting, the group directed its attention to three specific questions: What sorts of ministerial leadership and church life are needed in order to enable congregations and their leaders to be faithful to the demands of the gospel in the contemporary situation? What kinds of theological education are required for this leadership and church life? What relationships are needed between schools and churches in order to enable the development of faithful leadership?

Discussion of the first question reflected a broadly shared conviction that requisite for ministerial leadership is *theological* leadership, in two senses of that phrase: first, a leadership that is grounded in theological aptitude, that is, in a well-developed, well-honed capacity and inclination to pay attention to God and to the things of God; and second, a leadership intent upon sharing that theological aptitude with the community and cultivating it in the community. Theological leadership in both these senses is, the discussants observed, less a matter of technique than of character. It requires a blend of steadiness and flexibility. It also requires a sober realism concerning the extent of the world's (and the church's, and the self's) corruption, and concerning the fact that the exercise of leadership will bring with it an abundant measure of suffering, some of it merited, much of it undeserved.

Other requisites for ministerial leadership were seen to be rooted in this theological aptitude. The members of the consultation were clear that pastors and other leaders need various specific abilities—for example, the ability to plan an effective meeting, or to keep track of finances—which have nothing especially theological about them at first glance. But they resisted the notion that these specific abilities were in fact non-theological. They saw a problem in the widespread tendency to treat administration (to pick one example from the discussion) as a matter of technique rather than as a theological practice. Many rejected the entire concept of "management" as inappropriate in a discussion of pastoral responsibility, and were highly critical of attempts to import secular, technocratically-inspired resources into the church's thinking in this area. Others favored the adaptation and theological transformation of such resources. In this connection, some spoke of the *stewardship of institutions* as a significant responsibility of church leaders, a responsibility whose effective exercise demands an understanding of what is articulated in Christian doctrines of creation, sin, redemption, and so forth. Ecclesiastical institutions, they thought, are neither to be disparaged nor to be worshiped; they are to be de-idolized and affirmed in their proper place. Their maintenance and management is part of the vocation of leadership. While the participants agreed that church leaders have much to learn from competent non-theological studies of administration and leadership, at least some also suspected that theology might have some distinctive and useful things to contribute to the understanding of those fields.

As to the sorts of church life needed for faithfulness to the gospel, the discussion again focused on essentials. Churches must be marked by hospitality: welcoming all, and especially the stranger, in God's name. This kind of hospitality is very demanding of those who share in extending it. It requires not only time, effort, and material resources, but also and foremost an ongoing personal and communal transformation, a constant overcoming of the inhospitableness that lingers in the self and in the community and that is always eager to reassert itself. An important source of strength and encouragement in the task, so far as the participants in this consultation were concerned, is the "communion of saints," extended both historically and geographically: actual people and actual congregations that have borne witness in their own lives to the generosity of God. Still more important is a vital awareness of that same generosity in the transforming presence of the Holy Spirit.

When asked what kinds of theological education are required for these sorts of leadership and church life, the participants' answers revealed general agreement on a few central principles. First, the kinds of theological education we need are kinds that keep at the forefront the overall aim of equipping persons with theological aptitude, in its various dimensions and specifications. The members of the consultation did not find much promise in the conventional tendency to regard the interpretation of texts and traditions as belonging to the "theoretical" side of the curriculum, and to regard the work of attending to human situations (personal, cultural, etc.) as belonging to the "practical" side. Interpreting texts and interpreting, let us say, instances of social conflict both require specific abilities acquired in part through practice. Theological students practice reading texts and are guided in that practice. Similarly, they need (and sometimes get) practice under supervision in reading situations of various sorts. They need to be enabled to see the similarities and the connections between the two: for example, to read texts in their socio-cultural contexts, and to read situations in light of the texts which bear the community's wisdom. A theological education that concentrates on situational analysis and critique is no more adequate than one that deals exclusively with the practices of reading texts. What is needed is theological education that aims explicitly at developing in students the sort of holistic aptitude for paying attention that is basic to genuine church leadership.

Second, we need kinds of theological education that place themselves in a community of faith. While most of the discussants wanted to see the theological school itself as in some sense a community of faith, the difficulty of specifying the sense in which that is so was acknowledged. For some, the theological school is aptly described as a congregation or liturgical community; its own ecclesial identity is an important aspect of its life and work. This view has some implications for the question of who should belong to the school, as well as for the sorts of scholarship consistent with its life. Others would insist that the school is not itself a congregation, and does not have the mission of a congregation. On this view, the school may in some cases at least include among its members earnest seekers and skeptics as well as believers (whatever that latter term may mean). It may include members of quite disparate religious communities. The faith that makes it a community of faith may in some ways be quite distinct from the faith that makes a congregation a community of faith.

However this feature of the school's identity is sorted out, the discussants were reasonably clear that the theological school should be seen as a particular enterprise of the community or communities of faith, entrusted with a distinctive mission on their behalf and sustained by a living relationship to them. They were also clear that theological education itself requires some involvement of the learners in communities of faith beyond the school as sites for learning, and thus requires some sort of partnership between school and church.

This led to the third topic question: What relationships are needed between schools and churches to fulfill this aim? There was less consensus in an answer to this question than in most points in the discussion, perhaps because the participants were recalling a diversity of forms of such relationship, both good and bad, from their own experience. In any event, it was generally agreed that not all theological education for church leadership happens best in schools of theology. It is increasingly a common practice to blame the seminary for the failings of church leadership, if not of the church in general, and then to demand that the seminary do more, which means including more required courses in areas of perceived weakness as well as doing a better job overall. However, the educational process goes on before, alongside, and after the seminary experience. Some discussants suggested that it is very important for both the church and the school to ask themselves what aspects of education for church leadership are best accomplished in the context of the theological school, and what aspects are best addressed in other settings. Some, convinced that the school is not an effective context for learning practical reasoning, called for more movement away from the school toward the congregation and community as the site for education in the practices of church leadership. Others thought that to assign "book learning" to the school and "experiential learning" to the congregation or community in this way would strengthen prevalent obstacles to effective ministerial education and would hinder constructive relationships between church and school. They did not want to lose sight of points previously made concerning the overall aim of theological education and the necessary coinherence of its dimensions. They preferred to ask: How might the church and the school better cooperate in the realization of this common educational aim? Answering this question might, of course, involve drawing some distinctions between the tasks proper to each, but these distinctions should not, they felt, be drawn in advance of the discussion between church and school over these matters, and they might turn out to be quite different from what either party by itself might anticipate. For example, just as the church may need to find new ways of, in effect, "being a school" for its leaders, so the school may need to find new ways of "being ecclesial," that is, of nurturing Christian existence, helping people (students, staff, and faculty) learn to live together and care for one another, and making more explicit connections between the life of learning and the life of religious faith.

Some such hope for a discussion productive of new insights animated this consultation itself, and the hope was not disappointed.

9

REJOICING in the TRUTH

HISTORICALLY, METHODIST RATIONALES for continuing education for ministers, as for ministerial education in general, have tended toward the practical. Knowledge is meant to inform practice, and the value of knowledge is in its positive effects upon practice. A thoroughgoing practice-oriented approach to this subject might not only be in line with some characteristic tendencies of Methodist thought, but might also have real benefit. Informed by an adequate vision of what practices are and of what participation in a practice involves, such an approach might yield a very productive understanding of ongoing education for ministerial leadership.[1]

But practice-oriented approaches are not always so informed. At their worst, such practical rationales become merely technocratic: to "do ministry" is to deploy a set of

1. I am thinking here of the attention given to practices and practical judgment in recent social philosophy, especially since Alasdair MacIntyre's *After Virtue*. See, for example, Joseph Dunne, *Back to the Rough Ground*.

skills that can be learned more or less discretely (in intensive short-term training modules, say), and that can be refreshed or strengthened through further training. At their best, perhaps, practical rationales have historically embraced or at least verged upon a professional model for ministry. On such a model, the professional identity and professional competence of pastoral leaders and others in specialized ministry rest upon a body of specialized, role-specific knowledge, initially gained through an extensive educational process (e.g., a professional degree program) leading to initial certification. This knowledge base needs to be augmented constantly to take account of developments in the field and of changes in the context in which the profession is exercised. Here, the technocratic impulse is overcome at least to some extent by considerations of such things as professional identity and public responsibility, and by an awareness of the limits of professional knowledge and competence itself.[2]

Despite a number of difficulties with it, especially in face of the changing character of ministerial leadership today, I am not prepared simply to reject a professional model for ordained ministry—nor yet to embrace one wholeheartedly. I suspect that the work of church leadership is more than a profession in some respects, and less than a profession in others; but in any case there is, I think, much to be gained by thinking through the ways in which ministry and the (other) professions share common ground.[3] This is true not least when it comes to issues having to do with appropriate modes

2. For a thoughtful treatment of these issues, see May, *Beleaguered Rulers*.

3. See, e.g., Camenisch, "Clergy Ethics and the Professional Ethics Model."

Rejoicing in the Truth 137

of education for ministerial leadership, including continuing education.

Most of the major proposals for rethinking theological education that have been produced in the past couple of decades have not centered on a professional model. Indeed, they have avoided one, in order to ground the enterprise more deeply in the character of theology itself. The consequent reorientation of theological study has involved some new approaches to the nature and aims of education for church leadership, in which its likenesses to and differences from various sorts of professional education may be seen in new light.[4] In an early and influential contribution to this literature on theological study, Edward Farley observed that "[t]he more the external tasks themselves are focused on as the one and only *telos* of theological education, the less the minister becomes qualified to carry them out."[5] Variations on his observation can be found in recent treatments of professional training in other fields. The warning carries implications for continuing education as well as for one's initial preparation for service. It might well be worthwhile to trace out those implications for continuing education in ministry, in conversation with similar undertakings in other fields.

Interesting and productive as that might be, my aim in what follows is not to explore a professionally-oriented rationale for continuing education. It is instead to pursue a more radical and more comprehensive vision of the role of learning in ministerial leadership—a vision that might inform such more particular conversations and explorations. This vision

4. For an overview of these developments, see chapter 6, "Theological Education: Confessional and Public."

5. Farley, *Theologia*, 128.

is, I believe, thoroughly Wesleyan in character, though in developing it here I will be giving relatively little attention to Wesley's specific observations on either learning or ministry. My approach will require me instead to work out some relevant features of a Wesleyan understanding of church, ministry, and learning from still more elemental sources in Wesley's thought. We begin with what life is all about.

I.

In a Wesleyan understanding of us human beings, knowledge, like love and joy, is one of the things we are born for. Wesley's "presupposed theology," as John Deschner called it—the doctrinal substance that Wesley absorbed and appropriated, and that informed his preaching and practice—included the principle that the image of God in which we are created is a *triune* image, an *imago trinitatis*. We "correspond" to God in our God-given capacity to *know* God and God's creation, as well as in our capacities to *love* God and fellow-creature and to *rejoice* in what is thus known and loved. In our knowing, we respond to (or even, in a way, partake in) the intelligibility of God and of all that God has made; we resonate with the *Logos* that is one of the ways God is God, and that informs all of creation. In our loving, we respond to—or, better, find ourselves caught up into—the love of God, the love that God *is* and "that moves the sun and the other stars."[6] Our joy and thanksgiving are evoked by the sheer gift of all this, and are a response to its ultimate source in the reality of God. The

---

6. "My will and my desire were turned by love, / The love that moves the sun and the other stars"—the last lines of Dante's *Divine Comedy* (here in the Sayers-Reynolds translation).

relations among these three capacities—knowledge, love, and joy (or, with Charles Wesley, "wonder, love, and praise")—are relations of mutual indwelling and reciprocity that mirror in creaturely reality the *perichoresis* of the three Persons of the Trinity. Each requires and sustains the others. Their common exercise constitutes the freedom in which our lives find their fulfillment, their true end.[7]

At least, this is how things are supposed to be.

According to an early sermon of John Wesley's on the image of God,[8] in the state of integrity human understanding was "just," "swift," "clear," and "great." Apparently, we (or, rather, Adam and Eve) had no trouble apprehending and honoring reality: seeing things as they are, thinking clearly, and reaching sound judgments. They were eager to grow in knowledge; they delighted in the truth. In Wesley's reconstruction of the Eden scenario, it was not an inordinate thirst for knowledge that led our first parents astray. There is no suggestion in his account that they (and we) would have been better off had they only downplayed their intelligence, switched off their brains and asked no more questions. Their free choice of evil over good remains, for Wesley, a mystery; but there is the strong implication that if they had thought things through when the forbidden fruit was proffered, using the intelligence they had been given, they would not have sinned.[9]

7. I have sketched out Wesley's Trinitarian theology and anthropology a little further, but by no means extensively, in chapter 1, "Methodist Doctrine: An Understanding."

8. Wesley, "The Image of God," in Outler, *Sermons,* 4:292–303.

9. Wesley returns to the subject several decades later, in the sermon "On the Fall of Man," in Outler, *Sermons,* 2:400–412, to much the same effect.

The Fall devastated our capacity for knowledge, along with our capacity for love and for joy. Think of the opposites of those adjectives with which Wesley described human understanding in the state of integrity: now, post-Fall, our knowing is unjust, unclear, slow, and small. Rather than welcoming and delighting in reality, we fear it. We hide from it. We deny or distort the truth, constructing and cherishing lies in its place. We bear false witness against our neighbor. We suppress inconvenient facts, and subvert the processes of discovery that might bring us face to face with them. We create modes of inquiry that will (we hope) enable us to define and deal with reality on our terms, to make it serve our desires. Even if we should decide that we really want to see things as they are, our fears and our illusions generally get the best of us. We live, as Wesley says, in "ignorance and error," largely self-imposed.

God's remedy in Jesus Christ for this state of foolishness, lovelessness, and misery in which we find ourselves is a healing and restoration of those created capacities that have gone wrong, a healing that includes our renewal in knowledge. One aspect of the Holy Spirit's work in regeneration is "opening the eyes of our understanding."[10] A recovery of our intelligence proceeds along with the recovery of our capacities for true love and for true joy, and is inextricably linked with these. It is the disclosure of the reality and love of God in Christ that enables the opening of "the eyes of our understanding," and that simultaneously evokes our love and our delight. Had he known her work, Wesley might have recognized a kin-

---

10. Ibid., 410. As in common with Wesley's sermons, an interweaving of scriptural passages lies behind his wording, in this case Luke 24:45 and Ephesians 1:18.

ship in the writing of the thirteenth-century Beguine mystic Mechthild of Magdeburg, although she thought and wrote in a decidedly un-Wesleyan idiom:

> I cannot dance, Lord, unless you lead me.
> If you want me to leap with abandon,
> You must intone the song.
> Then I shall leap into love,
> From love into knowledge,
> From knowledge into enjoyment,
> And from enjoyment beyond all human
> sensation . . .[11]

In any case, it is clear that Wesley resonated strongly with Paul's statement in 1 Corinthians 13:6, binding the three together: "Love . . . rejoices in the truth."

Exemplifying and bearing witness to this possibility of "love rejoicing in the truth" is the task of the church.

II.

Discussion of the church is often helped if we keep in mind a distinction between two common references of the term "church."[12] One the one hand, "church" may be used to refer to the totality of those who are being saved, i.e., who, by the grace of God in Christ and in the Holy Spirit are being restored to right relationship with God and fellow creature. The church in this sense is the "community of salvation." On the other hand, "church" may be used to refer to the totality of those who *know* about this saving activity of God, and who are

---

11. Mechthild of Magdeburg, *The Flowing Light of the Godhead*, 59.

12. I am indebted to Schubert M. Ogden for the terms of this distinction.

bearing witness to it explicitly in word and action. The church in this sense is the "community of witness," or, if you prefer, the "sign-community."[13] Ideally, these two communities coincide, and in the fullness of time perhaps they will; but in our experience and history, they are probably best portrayed as overlapping. The community of salvation may be presumed to include many who are not part of the explicit community of witness, though they may in fact bear witness in other ways to the God we know in Jesus Christ, to their neighbors' benefit. At the same time, the community of witness may include persons who have not (yet) accepted the grace of salvation, or who have ceased to accept it. Further ambiguities mark both communities. The "community of salvation" is the totality of those who *are being* restored to their purpose in creation, as well as of those who (as the "communion of saints") *have been* so restored. And the "community of witness" bears more or less genuine and effective witness, depending on a great many factors. The theologian H. Richard Niebuhr's remark that "the line between church and world does not run between souls, but through each soul" could be applied with both these senses of "church" in mind.

At its best, the church as it is found in a local congregation, denomination, or ecclesial tradition is "church" in both these senses. It is a particular community in whose members the image of God is taking shape, and in which that process is being manifest in some explicit and public connection with the gospel. Paul's favorite image for the church—"the body of

---

13. The latter term is favored by the Roman Catholic theologian Juan Luis Segundo, building on the Second Vatican Council's portrayal of the church as a sacrament of the salvation of the whole world; see his *The Community Called Church*.

Christ"—seems meant to convey all this, as does his way of expressing what needs to happen among the "foolish Galatians": "My little children, for whom I am again in the pain of childbirth until Christ is formed in you . . ." (Gal 4:19). We might say the church is coming to be wherever, and to whatever extent, this renewal and manifestation is happening.

Part of what is going on wherever the church is happening is a recovery of reason: people are coming into their right minds. This is not easy or simple. It is a matter of loss or relinquishment, as well as of gain and enhancement. Coming into our right minds involves leaving behind the lies and distortions with which we have simultaneously comforted and trapped ourselves. It involves overcoming our fear of and consequent hostility toward the truth. Bad habits in our thinking need to be broken, and good ones learned. At the same time, this recovery of reason is a gift, intimately connected with the gift of the love that casts out fear (1 John 4:18).

Dealing with all this is a large part of the church's ministry of the Word. The ministry of the Word is not just about proclaiming the gospel.[14] It is also about being brought into a position to hear and understand the gospel, and then learning to convey that good news to others honestly in ways that offer some chance of their hearing and understanding as well. But it goes even more deeply than this. Basically, it is about being truthful. The church's ministry of the Word is the church's caring for the truth, and for human capacity not only to endure the truth but to flourish in it and to let it flourish. The church exercises its ministry of the Word as, individually and in community, its members recover by God's grace

---

14. It might also be true to say that it *is* just about proclaiming the gospel, with all that that entails.

their human vocation to understand and bear witness to the truth. Linked with a ministry of Sacrament which is about the rebirth and growth of joy and thanksgiving, and a ministry of Order which is about the rebirth and growth of active love toward God and neighbor, there is this ministry whose focus is the gift of understanding. Its typical expressions within the United Methodist history include such things as founding and supporting schools, colleges and universities, sustaining a publishing house, working to foster good conditions for intellectual growth in the public educational system and to insure educational opportunity for all, and defending freedom of inquiry, as well as providing an environment in the local congregation that encourages the renewal of the mind.

III.

As the reference to Word, Sacrament, and Order just now might imply, and for reasons that might also be obvious by now, I find this threefold scheme for the scope of the church's ministry not merely useful but compelling. It has a significant history and a cogent theological rationale. It enables us to see some connections between the church's ministry and a Christian account of such things as what human life is meant for, what has gone wrong with it, what God is doing about it, and what the church has to do with what God is doing. Furthermore, it is a point on which many different ecclesial traditions are apparently finding "convergence" (to use the term of the 1982 Lima document, *Baptism, Eucharist and Ministry*).[15] Not least in its favor, it is, I think, of great practical value as a guide to our thinking about the scope and

15. World Council of Churches, *Baptism, Eucharist, and Ministry*.

coherence of the church's ministry over the long haul and in any given situation. It was used to advantage (and definitely with an eye toward future possibilities of ecumenical rapport) in official United Methodist statements on ministry prior to 1996. It was then rather abruptly abandoned in the 1996 *Book of Discipline* and its terms incorporated into other configurations, in the attempt to establish separate spheres of responsibility for deacons and elders.

A discussion of the current ordering of ministry in the United Methodist Church is outside the purpose of this essay. Any such structure has its strengths and its liabilities, and it may take quite some time for the consequences of the 1996 legislation, both positive and negative, to become very clear to us. In the meantime, I think it would be unfortunate if we were to lose sight of the older triadic (or trinitarian) scheme just because it is absent from our current official language. Its value as a conceptual instrument for thinking comprehensively about ministry has not yet been exhausted. What I wish to sketch here by way of an understanding of ministerial leadership is compatible in principle with a great variety of polities, including some which do not recognize this terminology at all.

The first point to be made is that the ministry of Word, Sacrament, and Order is first of all the general ministry of the church. It is not to be identified simply with the specialized ministry of the ordained. Ordained ministry has this shape *because* it is the shape of the ministry of the whole community in which Christ is being formed, and ordained ministry exists to serve that.

A second, related point to be kept in mind is that Word, Sacrament, and Order are not to be regarded as separate functions. Although distinct, they cannot be separated. Each involves the others, "perichoretically." Further, they are not merely functions. They are perhaps closer to *practices* in a strict sense of the term, and as such each involves "knowing" and "being," as well as "doing."[16] In a way, this fact only underscores the point about their inseparability. There is a sense in which the church's ministry of the Word is centered on "knowing," its ministry of Sacrament on "being," and its ministry of Order on "doing." But there is a "being" and a "doing" pertinent to the ministry of the Word, and a similar relation of all three factors in each of the other aspects of ministry.

The task of the special ministry of church leadership, however it is configured or "ordered," is to assist the whole church to receive, affirm, and exercise its threefold ministerial vocation. The task of church leadership is not to minister on behalf of (or in place of) the people.[17] It is to empower and lead the people in ministry. In her preaching and teach-

16. On the concept of a practice in this connection, see Dykstra, "Reconceiving Practice." Among the relevant features of practices as Dykstra portrays them, drawing on the work of Alasdair McIntyre and others, are these: practices are cooperative and socially established; the goods they generate are inherent in the practice itself; and practices "bear epistemological weight," in that through them "we may come to awareness of certain *realities* that outside of these practices are beyond our ken" (45). On the triad of knowing, being, and doing in education for ministry, see Smith and Wood, "Learning Goals and the Assessment of Learning in Theological Schools."

17. There are circumstances in which it may be appropriate for an ordained minister to "represent" the church and to engage in some aspect of ministry explicitly on its behalf. These circumstances may, however, be more rare and more limited than we are at first inclined to think, influenced as we still are by the centuries-old model in which the "clergy" really *are* the church, and the "laity" the objects rather than the agents of ministry.

ing, for example, a pastoral minister is (we would hope) both exemplifying the ministry of the Word and equipping her hearers to carry it out themselves. She is helping them to become bearers, as well as hearers, of the Word. She is enabling them to develop an understanding of God and the gospel that is pertinent to their lives, and also helping them learn what it means to awaken understanding in others. Her leadership in this regard is effective insofar as both the substance and the manner of her teaching and preaching serve this complex end. This will require of her not only knowledge and skill but also a set of dispositions appropriate in one committed to "rejoicing in the truth." It will require in her habits of self-criticism, self-transcendence, hospitality to new information and new insights, and radical faith.

IV.

In light of these considerations having to do with the nature and aims of the church's ministry, perhaps the most apt form of continuing education for ministerial leadership is to participate with the laity in theological study. By theological study, I mean inquiry that is aimed at the knowledge of God, and at understanding everything else in relation to God. Theological study in this sense can have a vast range of particular "subjects" (the Bible, Christian doctrine, our country's foreign policy, human sexuality, religious diversity, etc.) and a correspondingly wide assortment of potential texts or other materials.

Teaching is often a very effective way to learn. This phenomenon is acknowledged across many fields, and it plays an increasingly important role in many formal programs of study, including many in theology. We often come to understand something more fully—whether the "something" is a concept, a principle, a hypothesis, or a historical event—by explaining it to someone else. Their questions, objections, tentative inferences and the like will often reveal the gaps in our own present understanding, will suggest new possibilities we hadn't considered, and will give us new ways of looking at the subject. We become teachers and learners together, engaged in a common inquiry into the subject matter. Good teaching often comes down to providing an environment and structure in which that sort of disciplined conversation can proceed. Opportunities for teaching become opportunities for learning, not only insofar as the one who is to teach must often extend or deepen his or her grasp of the subject beforehand so as to be able to teach, but also in that the event of teaching itself is an occasion for learning.

But it is not only on account of its effectiveness in this way that "learning by teaching" in a congregational setting is to be commended as a mode of continuing education for ministers. A still more important reason is its contribution to the general ministry of the church. When, for example, the pastor and the members of the congregation are engaged in theological inquiry together, sharing questions and insights with one another, they are building one another up in the ministry of the Word, and therefore in the other aspects of ministry as well. Not only are they learning about whatever the particular subject matter may be—a doctrine, a biblical text, an issue in social ethics—they are learning how to learn and how to teach, and in their interaction with one another and with the subject matter they are learning and strengthening the dispositions required in a life that honors the truth.

Carried out in this way, in this context, the pastor's learning is itself an engagement in ministerial leadership.

There are other forms and other contexts of learning—in solitude, with colleagues, in formal academic programs—and these are not to be neglected. Each is valuable in its own way, and each may be more suitable than the congregational setting for certain educational purposes. However, leading the congregation in theological study is both an uncommonly rich and an unduly neglected opportunity in learning, and one that might commend itself particularly to the people called Methodists.

BIBLIOGRAPHY

Abraham, William J., et al. (General Commission on Christian Unity and Interreligious Concerns). "In Search of Unity: A Conversation with Recommendations for the Unity of The United Methodist Church." Report from the Dialogue on Theological Diversity within the United Methodist Church, Nashville, November 20–21, 1997, and Dallas, February 19–20, 1998. Online: http://www.gccuic-umc.org/web/webpdf/unity.pdf.

Alighieri, Dante. *The Divine Comedy 3: Paradise*. Translated by Dorothy L. Sayers and Barbara Reynolds. New York: Penguin, 2004.

Austin, J. L. *How to Do Things with Words*. Edited by J. O. Urmson. The William James Lectures, 1955. New York: Oxford University Press, 1962.

Babcock, William S. "A Changing of the Christian God: The Doctrine of the Trinity in the Seventeenth Century." *Interpretation* 45 (1991) 133–46.

Baker, Frank, editor. *Letters I*. The Oxford Edition of the Works of John Wesley 25. Oxford: Oxford University Press, 1980.

Barth, Karl. *Church Dogmatics* I/1. Edited by G. W. Bromiley and T. F. Torrance. Translated by G. W. Bromiley. Edinburgh: T. & T. Clark, 1975.

British Council of Churches. *The Report of the BCC Study Commission on Trinitarian Doctrine Today*. Vol 1. of *The Forgotten Trinity*. London: British Council of Churches, 1989.

Buckley, Michael J. *At the Origins of Modern Atheism*. New Haven, CT: Yale University Press, 1987.

Bulletin of the Association of Theological Schools in the United States and Canada 42.3 (1996).

Bultmann, Rudolf. *Theologische Enzyklopädie*. Edited by Eberhard Jüngel and Klaus W. Müller. Tübingen: Mohr/Siebeck, 1984.

Camenisch, Paul F. "Clergy Ethics and the Professional Ethics Model." In *Clergy Ethics in a Changing Society*, edited by James P. Wind et al., 114–33. Louisville, KY: Westminster John Knox, 1991.

Christian, William A., Sr. *Doctrines of Religious Communities: A Philosophical Study*. New Haven, CT: Yale University Press, 1987.

Cragg, Gerald R. *From Puritanism to the Age of Reason: A Study of Changes in Religious Thought within the Church of England, 1660 to 1700*. Cambridge: Cambridge University Press, 1950.

———, editor. *The Appeals to Men of Reason and Religion, and Certain Related Open Letters*. The Oxford Edition of the Works of John Wesley 11. Oxford: Oxford University Press, 1975.

De George, Richard T. *The Nature and Limits of Authority*. Lawrence: University Press of Kansas, 1985.

Deschner, John. *Wesley's Christology: An Interpretation*. 2nd ed. Dallas, TX: Southern Methodist University Press, 1985.

Dunne, Joseph. *Back to the Rough Ground: Practical Judgment and the Lure of Technique*. Notre Dame, IN: University of Notre Dame Press, 1993.

Dykstra, Craig L. "Reconceiving Practice." In *Shifting Boundaries: Contextual Approaches to the Study of Theological Education*, edited by Barbara G. Wheeler and Edward Farley, 35–66. Louisville, KY: Westminster John Knox, 1991.

Edwards, John R. *Multilingualism* London: Penguin, 1995.

"Evangelicals call for move to higher ground." United Methodist News Service release, March 8, 2000. Online: http://archives.umc.org/umns/news_archive2000.asp?ptid=2&story={A9794361-8797-4E11-9098-04A5E8A0DDA5}&mid=3366.

Fackre, Gabriel. "Educating the Church." In *Theological Education in the Evangelical Tradition*, edited by D. G. Hart and R. Albert Mohler Jr., 275–77. Grand Rapids: Baker, 1996.

Farley, Edward. *Theologia: The Fragmentation and Unity of Theological Education*. Philadelphia: Fortress, 1983.

Friedrich, Carl J. "Authority, Reason, and Discretion." In *Authority*, edited by Carl J. Friedrich for the American Society of Political and Legal Philosophy, 28–48. Nomos 1. Cambridge: Harvard University Press, 1958.

Gilpin, W. Clark. "Basic Issues in Theological Education: A Selected Bibliography." *Theological Education* 25 (1989) 115–21.

Gustafson, James M. Introduction to *The Responsible Self*, by H. Richard Niebuhr, 6–41. New York: Harper & Row, 1963.

Heitzenrater, Richard Paul. "John Wesley and the Oxford Methodists, 1725–35." Ph.D. diss., Duke University, 1972.

Heppe, Heinrich. *Die Dogmatik der evangelisch-reformierten Kirche dargestellt und aus den Quellen belegt*. Edited by Ernst Bizer. Neukirchen: Moers, 1935. Translated by G. T. Thomson as *Reformed Dogmatics*. Grand Rapids: Baker, 1978.

Hunter, J. F. M. *Essays after Wittgenstein*. Toronto: University of Toronto Press, 1973.

Jones, William. *The Catholic Doctrine of a Trinity: Proved by Above an Hundred Short and Clear Arguments*. London: Rivington, 1801.

Jüngel, Eberhard. *Glauben und Verstehen: Zum Theologiebegriff Rudolf Bultmanns*. Heidelberg: Winter, 1985.

Kasper, Walter. *The God of Jesus Christ*. Translated by Matthew J. O'Connell. New York: Crossroad, 1986.

Keller, Evelyn Fox. *A Feeling for the Organism: The Life and Work of Barbara McClintock*. New York: Freeman, 1983.

Kelsey, David H. *Between Athens and Berlin: The Theological Education Debate*. Grand Rapids: Eerdmans, 1993.

———. *The Uses of Scripture in Recent Theology*. Philadelphia: Fortress, 1975.

———. *To Understand God Truly: What's Theological about a Theological School*. Louisville: Westminster John Knox, 1992.

Kelsey, David H., and Barbara G. Wheeler. "Thinking About Theological Education: The Implications of 'Issues Research' for Criteria of Faculty Excellence." *Theological Education* 28 (1991) 11–26.

Klaiber, Walter, and Manfred Marquardt. *Gelebte Gnade: Grundriss einer Theologie der Evangelisch-methodistischen Kirche*. Stuttgart: Christliches Verlagshaus, 1993.

Lash, Nicholas. *The Beginning and the End of "Religion."* Cambridge: Cambridge University Press, 1996.

———. *Believing Three Ways in One God: A Reading of the Apostles' Creed*. Notre Dame, IN: University of Notre Dame Press, 1992.

Lindbeck, George A. *The Nature of Doctrine: Religion and Theology in a Postliberal Age*. Philadelphia: Westminster, 1984.

Luther, Martin. *D. Martin Luthers Werke*. Kritische Gesamtausgabe. Weimar: Böhlau, 1883–.

MacIntyre, Alasdair. *After Virtue*. Notre Dame, IN: University of Notre Dame Press, 1981.

Maddox, Randy. "Opinion, Religion, and 'Catholic Spirit': John Wesley on Theological Integrity." *Asbury Theological Journal* 47 (1992) 63–87.

May, William F. *Beleaguered Rulers: The Public Obligation of the Professional*. Louisville: Westminster John Knox, 2001.

Mechthild of Magdeburg. *The Flowing Light of the Godhead*. Translated by Frank Tobin. New York: Paulist, 1998.

Mohler, R. Albert, Jr. "Thinking of the Future." In *Theological Education in the Evangelical Tradition*, edited by D. G. Hart and R. Albert Mohler Jr., 278–83. Grand Rapids: Baker, 1996.

Moltmann, Jürgen. *Der Geist des Lebens: Eine ganzheitliche Pneumatologie*. Munich: Kaiser, 1991.

Morse, Christopher. *Not Every Spirit: A Dogmatics of Christian Disbelief*. Valley Forge, PA: Trinity, 1994.

Muller, Richard A. *Post-Reformation Reformed Dogmatics*. Vol. 2. Grand Rapids: Baker, 1993.

Niebuhr, H. Richard. *The Meaning of Revelation*. New York: Macmillan, 1941, 1960.

Ogden, Schubert M. "Doctrinal Standards in the United Methodist Church." In *Doctrine and Theology in the United Methodist Church*, edited by Thomas A. Langford, 39–51. Nashville, TN: Kingswood, 1991.

Outler, Albert C., editor. *Sermons*. The Works of John Wesley 1–4. Nashville: Abingdon, 1984–1987.

Peters, R. S. "Symposium: Authority." *Proceedings of the Aristotelian Society*, Supplementary Volume 32 (1958) 207–24.

Pillow, Thomas Wright. "John Wesley's Doctrine of the Trinity." *The Cumberland Seminarian* 24 (1986) 1–10.

Placher, William C. "The Nature of Biblical Authority: Issues and Models from Recent Theology." In *Conservative, Moderate, Liberal: The Biblical Authority Debate*, edited by Charles R. Blaisdell, 1–19. St. Louis: CBP, 1989.

Pöhlmann, Horst Georg. *Abriss der Dogmatik*. 2nd ed. Gütersloh: Gütersloher/Mohn, 1975.

Preus, Robert J. *The Theology of Post-Reformation Lutheranism: A Study of Theological Prolegomena*. St. Louis: Concordia, 1970.

Schmid, Heinrich. *Die Dogmatik der evangelisch-lutherischen Kirche dargestellt und aus den Quellen belegt*. Edited by Horst Georg Pöhlmann. 10th ed. Gütersloh: Gütersloher/Mohn, 1983. Translated by Charles A. Hay and Henry E. Jacobs as *The Doctrinal Theology of the Evangelical Lutheran Church*. Minneapolis: Augsburg, 1961.

Scroggs, Robin. "The Bible as Foundational Document," *Interpretation* 49 (1995) 17–30.

Segundo, Juan Luis. *The Community Called Church*. Translated by John Drury. A Theology for Artisans of a New Humanity 1. Maryknoll, NY: Orbis, 1973.

"Sherlock, William." In *The Dictionary of National Biography*, edited by Sir Leslie Stephen and Sir Sidney Lee, 18:95–97. Oxford: Oxford University Press, 1960.

Smith, Gordon T., and Charles M. Wood. "Learning Goals and the Assessment of Learning in Theological Schools." *Theological Education* 39 (2003) 17–29.

Telford, John, editor. *The Letters of the Rev. John Wesley*. Vol. 6. London: Epworth, 1931.

Torrance, Thomas F. *The Ground and Grammar of Theology*. Charlottesville: University Press of Virginia, 1980.

Turretin, Francis. *Institutes of Elenctic Theology*. Translated by George Musgrave Giger, edited by James T. Dennison Jr. 3 vols. Phillipsburg, NJ: P. & R. Publishing, 1992.

United Methodist Church (U.S.). *The Book of Discipline of the United Methodist Church*. Nashville: United Methodist Publishing House, 1988.

———. *The Book of Discipline of the United Methodist Church*. Nashville: United Methodist Publishing House, 1996.

Wainwright, Geoffrey. "Why Wesley Was a Trinitarian." *The Drew Gateway* 59.2 (1990) 26–43.

Watt, E. D. *Authority*. New York: St. Martin's, 1982.

Wesley, John. *Explanatory Notes upon the New Testament*. London: Epworth, 1950.

Wittgenstein, Ludwig. *Philosophical Investigations*. 3rd ed. Translated by G. E. M. Anscombe. New York: Macmillan, 1958.

Wood, Charles M. *An Invitation to Theological Study*. Valley Forge, PA: Trinity, 1994.

———. *Vision and Discernment: An Orientation in Christian Theology*. Scholars Press Studies in Theological Education. Decatur, GA: Scholars, 1985.

Wood, Charles M., and Ellen Blue. *Attentive to God: Thinking Theologically in Ministry*. Nashville, TN: Abingdon, 2008.

World Council of Churches. *Baptism, Eucharist and Ministry*. Faith and Order Paper 111. Geneva: World Council of Churches, 1982.

www.ingramcontent.com/pod-product-compliance
Lightning Source LLC
Chambersburg PA
CBHW022119160426
43197CB00009B/1086